MW01289675

The Carmichael Prayerbook

spiritual devotions adapted from traditional Gaelic prayers
collected in Alexander Carmichael's *Carmina Gadelica*

Prepared by
Timothy J. Ray

ISBN: 9781719987141

One generation shall laud your works to another,
and shall declare your mighty acts.

Psalm 145: 4

Table of Contents

Preface

Creative projects — including spiritual activities — have a way of acquiring a life of their own, going in their own directions and making demands that were never anticipated at their conception. This certainly was the case with my *A Journey to the Land of the Saints*, a series of spiritual exercises based on the journey of Saint Brendan the Navigator. I initially intended this project to be an ecumenical retreat offered at churches and retreat houses conducted by different Christian denominations. With this in mind, I planned to use the different prayer services and liturgies of each community to introduce the topics of the retreat, but this soon proved impractical and I needed to choose another way of proceeding with my project.

This challenge led me to develop a series of prayer services using the traditional Gaelic prayers collected in Alexander Carmichael's *Carmina Gadelica*. Even in translation, the Scottish prayers gathered in Carmichael's collection have a potent immediacy that allows a person praying them in the present to hear the voice of past generations united by their desire for union with God. I often returned to the *Carmina Gadelica* for my own spiritual nourishment over the last decade or so and I wanted to preserve the simplicity of these often very short prayers in the services I created, hoping that the modern participants in my retreat might feel their own voices merge with the men and women who spoke these prayers over the centuries.

The initial appeal of these services among my friends and colleagues — whether serving God as pastors of churches, as spiritual directors or as theologians — validated my efforts and I soon realized I had a valuable resource that would enrich my spiritual practice. By including options that were not needed for the services presented in *A Journey to the Land of the Saints*, I created a highly flexible structure for group prayer that speaks to a broad ecumenical audience. So, I decided to incorporate this prayer service — what I have come to call the Carmichael Liturgy — into my spiritual formation work with others as well as into my continuing explorations of the affinities between Celtic and Ignatian spirituality.

Recognizing that my explorations of the *Carmina Gadelica* might help other individuals or groups seeking Celtic resources for their own prayer and worship, I decided to publish the Carmichael Liturgy and some of the other prayers I have developed using this collection over the years. Since the language in Alexander Carmichael's translations may occasionally distract modern readers from the intimate expressions of personal faith his collection gathers, I needed to revise some wording from the original prayers to reflect contemporary English usage. Still, it remains my hope that the materials in this book preserve the eloquent testimony of the Gaelic folk prayers gathered by Alexander Carmichael and allow pilgrims — both past and present — to join their voices in prayer.

Thanks and Acknowledgements

Special thanks to J. L. Chapman, Bernard Colonna, John Dale, Kathleen Deignan, Edward Egros, Rosalyn Knowles Ferrell, Ruben Habito, Patrick Henry, Per Mollerup, Susan Rakoczy, Brian Ramsay, James Swonger and David Teschner. Each of these friends contributed in a unique way to the development of the prayers offered in this collection.

Also, thanks to the Division of Christian Education of the National Council of the Churches of Christ in the United States of America for permission to use the biblical citations excerpted in the Carmichael Liturgy from the *New Revised Standard Version Bible: with the Apocrypha* (New York: Harper Bibles, 1989).

Finally, thanks to the archives of the University of Edinburgh for providing the public domain portrait of Alexander Carmichael by William Skeoch Cumming used on the cover of this book.

In addition, it is important to acknowledge that the materials gathered in this book were adapted from Alexander Carmichael's compilation of Gaelic prayers published in *Carmina Gadelica: Hymns and Incantations* (Edinburgh: Floris Books, 1992). While Carmichael's collection is in the public domain, this edition remains an invaluable spiritual resource that deserves proper recognition.

Introduction

The prayers collected in Alexander Carmichael's *Carmina Gadelica* encompassed every aspect of the lives of the people who initially invoked them. They understood God was present in every aspect of their lives from the beginning of morning until the end of evening, so they acknowledged and gave thanks for the Divine Presence shaping and sustaining their activities — including returning their dead to God — in every moment of the day. Then, as they prepared to sleep, these men and women prayed for God's protection when they were most vulnerable and unable to protect themselves. In this way, they nurtured a life in harmony with Paul's admonition in 1 Thessalonians 5: 16-18 that Christians "Rejoice always, pray without ceasing, [and] give thanks in all circumstances."

While many of these prayers address activities now alien to us, such as smooring (or covering) a fire at night, we still should aspire to share in the fundamental disposition of faith expressed by these spiritual forebears. Like them, we need to recognize and express gratitude for God's presence in our own lives — opening ourselves to the Divine Presence that gives our lives meaning and purpose. While we should not simply mimic the prayers of men and women from the past, we can find inspiration in the words and rhythms of their language to form more general prayers intended to help us become more comfortable in expressing both our needs and our gratitude as we recognize the presence of God surrounding us in every moment and activity of our lives.

So, with this in mind, this prayerbook looks to Alexander Carmichael's collection to find language intended to illumine our own spiritual condition and to inflame our own spiritual fervor. It offers three types of ecumenical prayers and spiritual devotions well-suited to our own time, needs and desires. First, it provides a contemplative prayer service using the words of the *Carmina Gadelica* to create a foundation for communal worship. Second, it presents a collection of prayer sequences based on selections from Carmichael's collection intended to help individuals or groups foster a deeper awareness of God's presence in their lives. Third, and finally, it proposes devotional exercises using discrete prayers from the *Carmina Gadelica* designed to foster increased awareness of God's presence in our daily life and to encourage the habit of continual and ongoing prayer.

The Carmichael Liturgy

This ecumenical prayer service weaves together prayers from the *Carmina Gadelica* to create a distinctive and flexible expression of common worship. The liturgy includes elements familiar to most Christian communities, making it familiar and accessible to members of different religious denominations. But the rhythms and language of the service preserve its distinguishing characteristics, welcoming and challenging communities to blend their voices with the generations of men and women who first prayed the words woven into the liturgy.

The Carmichael Liturgy offers a wide range of options in terms of content and style of presentation, creating a highly flexible structure for communal worship. The service contains various options for the penitential prayers, petitionary prayers and final blessing so that it may be shaped by the needs and desires of people participating in it. The service also provides groups with the choice of deciding how much silence or music is appropriate for their community's needs. In addition, the readings in the service may focus on a particular theme or event of particular interest to the congregation or follow the general seasons and cycles of the denomination using it. Finally, the optional Eucharistic prayer allows the community to create different levels of worship at different times.

Note: The considerations at the beginning of the section containing the Carmichael Liturgy examine these various options in detail. With this in mind, it will be important to decide which elements best suit each particular group of worshipers.

Another concern that needs to be addressed before conducting the Carmichael Liturgy involves leadership and group participation. The liturgy contains options for general participation — such as sharing thoughts on the readings after the Gospel or in offering personal prayers during the service — that make it appropriate for small prayer groups. But the service also is well-suited for large congregations, although it will be necessary to provide clearer boundaries for group participation as the number of people involved in the prayer services increases (e.g., singing, offering personal petitions during the service, etc.). So, it will be helpful to consider the type of leadership role that fosters the communal experience desired in these different times of worship.

The Prayer Sequences

These sequences serve as reminders of the graces desired from God to face the rigors of daily life, but they also echo the prayers found in the Carmichael Liturgy. With this in mind, these prayers are designed to focus on specific times and spiritual dispositions. The first two sequences serve as morning and night prayers, remaining general in tone. But the rest of the prayers have a thematic core organized around a particular grace or need — the things desired from God so that a person may manifest the Divine Presence in his or her life (e.g., the courage to give witness, the need for protection in challenging times, consolation in sorrow, etc.).

Written in the first person, these prayers may be used discretely by individuals or by a community. When used alone in private prayer, these sequences allow individuals to bring their personal desires and needs before God. When these prayers are used in community with others, however, single and solitary voices come together in an expression of shared aspiration that echoes the psalms of the Bible. In either case, the individuals or groups using these sequences should take time to read through them before their prayer — including the readings and any songs they will use — so the desires expressed in the prayers may take root in their hearts and make space for the special graces that God will provide to them.

The sequences also may be coordinated to the Carmichael Liturgy. If a community gathers for the liturgy on an occasional basis, individuals or small groups might decide to use these prayers to highlight individual needs and desires that could be brought to the larger community when it next gathers for common worship. However, if a community uses the Carmichael Liturgy daily (as a morning or evening prayer), individuals or groups may decide to complement this shared prayer with the simpler sequences by using them during another part of the day devoted to private needs and desires. However, if using these prayer sequences with the Carmichael Liturgy, care should be taken to avoid making these prayers burdensome or tiring.

Note: Before approaching these prayers — in the manner considered best by the individual or group using them — it will be important to take into account the considerations at the beginning of the section of this prayerbook devoted to the prayer sequences.

The Devotional Exercises

These devotional exercises incorporate discrete prayers from the *Carmina Gadelica* into spiritual practices from other spiritual traditions. The first two — a preview and a review of the day (called examens) — come from the spiritual teachings of the Spanish mystic Ignatius of Loyola, who developed this prayer to heighten a person's awareness of God's presence in the commonplace experiences of daily life. On the other hand, the remaining exercises (a Gaelic prayer cycle for use with a prayer rope or with Anglican prayer beads) draw upon the Eastern Orthodox Christian tradition of repeating a short petitionary prayer while fingering the successive knots on a cord — ultimately as a semi-conscious action without planning or deliberation — to fulfill the admonition in 1 Thessalonians 5: 17 to "pray without ceasing".

The examens, which require 10 or 15 minutes each to complete, are intended to be used during the morning and in the evening. The morning examen should focus on the coming day, allowing the person to ask for God's guidance, protection and wisdom during future meetings and activities. The evening examen looks backward, eliciting gratitude for God's gifts during the day and heightening the individual's awareness of those moments inviting repentance and a desire for personal change. With this in mind, these two prayers are meant to be done together so they may complement each other. By balancing a cautious anticipation of a new morning with the realistic awareness of human frailty in the evening, they teach us to reach out confidently to God for love, care and forgiveness.

The prayer cycles provide a flexible tool for cultivating devotional constancy using discrete prayers from the *Carmina Gadelica*. They begin with the person expressing a humble desire to serve God while relying entirely on the Divine Presence for care and sustenance. Then, while moving from one knot or bead to another, the individual repeats a short petitionary sequence asking for protection, guidance or forgiveness. Finally, the person repeats the prayers from the beginning of the exercise again before finishing the devotion. Since the process of repeating the petitionary sequences may be repeated as often as the individual desires, this exercise may be used for short periods of quiet prayer or during long periods when the person wishes to prayer while engaged in other activities.

The Resources

The resources section at the end of this book provides suggestions intended to enrich both private prayer and community worship. To help individuals and groups select readings for the Carmichael Liturgy and the prayer sequences, there is a consideration of reading cycles developed by different Christian denominations and various approaches to selecting biblical readings (as well as specific concerns associated with choosing reflective materials for the Carmichael Liturgy's prelude). This is followed by a discussion of how to find and present music during the Carmichael Liturgy and prayer sequences. Finally, "On Holy Ground" presents three short rituals using prayers from Alexander Carmichael's *Carmina Gadelica* designed to foster a sacred space for individual prayer, particularly the prayer sequences or the devotional exercises in this prayerbook.

In whatever manner the prayers and devotions offered in this book are approached, they serve as reminders that God is waiting there to nurture and guide his creatures. So, it is important the match this generous and loving presence by being open to the many graces that will be bestowed through these spiritual exercises. Hopefully, the individuals and communities using this prayerbook will find inspiration in the words spoken by the men and women whose prayers are collected in the *Carmina Gadelica*. In this way, the example of these spiritual forebears will inspire modern men and women to find joy in their discovery of God's sustaining activity in the events and people of their own lives.

The Carmichael Liturgy

an ecumenical prayer service

Considerations

The Carmichael Liturgy offers a wide range of options, allowing communities to adapt it their particular needs and desires. Depending on the various elements you choose to include in it (e.g., Eucharist, silence, music, etc.), the service may range from thirty minutes to an hour in length. Therefore, while preparing to present the service, it will be important to reflect on the following issues:

• Silence

These services are intended to be contemplative in nature and contain a number of invitations to silent prayer, but people have different tolerances and capacities for silence. So, it will be important to assess the community's comfort level when deciding the amount of silence to include in the service.

• Music, for Meditation and Song

Music may be used during meditative periods instead of silence. If this is the case, the music should be presented in a seamless manner that does not distract the community from its reflections. Also, it will be necessary to decide whether musicians will perform the music or it will be presented through recordings.

In addition to the music used for meditation, music might contribute to your community's experience of the Carmichael Liturgy. If a community is large enough to support singing, it would be helpful to consult the suggestions in "Using Music with the Liturgy and Sequences" in the Resources Section of this prayerbook.

• Reflective Readings and Music

During the prelude to the Carmichael Liturgy, a reading or musical selection should be presented that guides the community into reflective prayer — allowing the members of the community to listen reflectively to these selections without being distracted by their presentation.

Suggestions concerning a reflective reading may be found in "Selecting Readings for the Liturgy and Sequences" in the Resources Section of this prayerbook, and suggestions concerning music are offered in "Using Music with the Liturgy and Sequences".

• Scriptural Readings

The scriptural readings in the Carmichael Liturgy may be selected to address a particular theme if it is presented on a special occasion or they may be coordinated to the cycle of readings used by a particular community or denomination. Suggestions concerning the selection of scriptural readings and psalms may be found in "Selecting Readings for the Liturgy and Sequences" in the Resources Section of this prayerbook.

Also, this prayer service uses a conversational tone in deference to the language found in the *Carmina Gadelica*, so it includes selections from the New Revised Standard Version Bible. This translation or another contemporary version of the Bible is highly recommended for the scriptural reading and psalm during the service. However, if a community is more comfortable with an older translation, it may wish to use the Authorized Version for the Gospel readings and the Scottish Metrical Psalter for the psalms (which also will preserve the Gaelic quality of the services).

• The Place of Worship

While this prayer service may be presented in a church with a large congregation, it is meant to be welcoming in character and expression. So, when used by a smaller prayer group, it would be helpful to present the Carmichael Liturgy in an intimate space — such as a small chapel, a prayer room in a church, or a room in a home — that offers a meditative focal point (e.g., a Celtic cross, icon or statue) and muted lighting (perhaps candlelight) to help the participants in the their prayer.

• The Eucharistic Prayer

If the Eucharistic Prayer is included in the Carmichael Liturgy, a member of the clergy will need to consecrate the elements during the service (or prior to it). So, it will be important to decide how to preserve them in a respectful manner during the course of the service. With this in mind, you may want to place the Eucharistic elements in a small tabernacle or (depending on the spiritual tradition of the community conducting the service) place them near the focal point of the chapel or prayer room until they are needed during communion.

The members of the community enter and pray in silence. After the community is fully assembled, the prelude should be presented.

Prelude

While maintaining a contemplative atmosphere, a brief reading or song is presented to the community. A period of silent meditation follows the selection's presentation before the leader begins the penitential prayers.

Penitential Prayers

A bell rings and the members of the community kneel. If anyone cannot kneel, they should remain seated with their heads bowed.

Leader	We bend our knees
All	*(making the sign of the cross)*
	in the eye of the Father who created us,
	in the eye of the Son who purchased us,
	in the eye of the Spirit who cleansed us. Amen.

All stand.

Leader	Lord Jesus Christ,
	give us the grace of repentance;
	give us the grace of earnestness;
	give us the grace of submission.
Community	**Give us the strength and courage to confess our guilt**
	as earnestly as were this the moment of our death.

If necessary, the leader announces the Petition of Mercy selected for the prayer service before continuing.

Option A

Leader	Lord Jesus,
	you are shade to those in the heat;
	you are shelter to those in the cold;

	you are a well to those in the desert.
	Lord Jesus, have mercy on us.
Community	**Lord Jesus, have mercy on us.**
Leader	Christ Jesus,
	you are eyes to those who are blind;
	you are ears to those who are deaf;
	you are health to those who are ailing.
	Christ Jesus, have mercy on us.
Community	**Christ Jesus, have mercy on us.**
Leader	Lord Jesus,
	you are the joy of all joyous things;
	you are the beam of the sun in the day;
	you are the guiding star in the night.
	Lord Jesus, have mercy on us.
Community	**Lord Jesus, have mercy on us.**

Proceed to the Penitential Prayer Sequence beginning "Lord Jesus Christ …" found after Option C.

Option B

Leader	Lord Jesus,
	help us speak according to your justice,
	help us heed your laws and directives.
	Each day and night, help us know your chastening,
	so we may act justly toward you and toward others.
	Lord Jesus, have mercy on us.
Community	**Lord Jesus, have mercy on us.**
Leader	Christ Jesus,
	help us count the causes of your mercy,
	help us praise the features of your goodness.
	Each day and night, help us know your kindness,
	so we may act tenderly toward you and toward others.
	Christ Jesus, have mercy on us.
Community	**Christ Jesus, have mercy on us.**
Leader	Lord Jesus,
	help us know the depths of your love,
	help us live according to your wisdom.
	Each day and night, help us know your peace,
	so we may act humbly toward you and toward others.

| | Lord Jesus, have mercy on us. |
| Community | **Lord Jesus, have mercy on us.** |

Proceed to the Penitential Prayer Sequence beginning "Lord Jesus Christ ..." found after Option C.

Option C

Leader	Lord Jesus,
	Bless and protect us beneath your glorious mantle.
	There is no plant in the ground, nor form in the strand,
	that is not full of your virtue.
	Lord Jesus, have mercy on us.
Community	**Lord Jesus, have mercy on us.**
Leader	Christ Jesus,
	Guard and secure us behind the strength of your shield,
	There is no life, in the sea or river, in air or on land,
	that does not proclaim your goodness.
	Christ Jesus, have mercy on us.
Community	**Christ Jesus, have mercy on us.**
Leader	Lord Jesus,
	Help and teach us to trust in your constant care.
	There is nothing in the firmament, nor beneath sun and moon,
	that is not full of your blessing.
	Lord Jesus, have mercy on us.
Community	**Lord Jesus, have mercy on us.**

The leader continues.

Leader	Lord Jesus Christ,
	with the Father who created us and the Spirit that cleansed us,
	Purify our hearts, make holy our souls and confirm our faith,
	keep safe our minds and compass our bodies all about.
	Enfold us...
Community	**... and surround us.**
Leader	Guide our speech...

Community	**… and our thoughts.**
Leader	Guard us in our sleeping…
Community	**… and in our waking.**
Leader	Nurture us in our watching…
Community	**… and in our hoping.**
Leader	Shield us in our lives…
Community	**… and grant us peace in eternity.**
Leader	Holy God,
	Father, Son and Spirit,
	pour down upon us from heaven
	the rich blessing of your forgiveness.
	Be patient with us and grant to us
	the fear of God, the love of God, and your affection
	so we may do your will on earth at all times …
Community	**… as the angels and saints do in heaven.**
Leader	Holy God,
	Father, Son and Spirit,
	pour down upon us from heaven
	the rich blessing of your peace.
	Peace between nations …
Community	**… peace between neighbors.**
Leader	Peace between kindred …
Community	**… peace between lovers.**
Leader	Peace between persons injured …
Community	**… peace between foes.**
Leader	Holy God,
	Father, Son and Spirit,
	help us to love and bless your creation,
	all that we see, all that we hear, all that we touch.
	Let us share your peace with our fellow creatures at all times,
	living as signs of forgiveness and reconciliation on the earth …
All	**… as the angels and saints do in heaven:**
	without malice, without jealousy, without envy,
	without fear, without terror of anyone under the sun.
	And may the Father, the Son and the Spirit
	kindle in our hearts the flame of love to our neighbors,
	to our foes, to our friends, to our kindred all,
	to the brave, to the knave, to the thrall.

Leader	The peace of the Father of Joy,
	the peace of Christ the Lamb,
	the peace of the Spirit of Grace, be with you.
Community	**The peace of the Father of Joy,**
	of Christ the Lamb, and of the Spirit of Grace,
	be with us all.
Leader	Let us share a sign of peace with those present here
	as a testimony to the peace God offers to the world.

The members of the community share a sign of peace before sitting down. A brief period of silence follows before the reader begins the Word of God.

The Word of God

The Gospel

Reader	I set the teachings of Christ before you;
	I set the guarding of God about you.
Community	**May it possess us and protect us all.**

Reader	A reading from the Gospel according to…

After indicating the source of the Gospel and reading the scriptural selection, the reader pauses for a moment before continuing.

	The gospel of Jesus Christ, source of strength,
	Source of salvation, source of healing grace.
Community	**May it be a mantle to our bodies.**

The Psalm

A brief silence follows the reading. Then, if necessary, the leader announces the psalm selected for the prayer service and the manner in which it will be recited before saying:

Leader	Let us praise God.

The community recites the psalm, in unison or antiphonally. Then, there is a brief period of silence before the reflection.

The Reflection

Depending upon the size of the prayer community, one of the following options should be chosen for the reflection:

• In a large group, in which it would be difficult for all participants to contribute equally, there is a brief silence after the psalm before an individual from the community (either the prayer leader or another person) presents a brief reflection on the scripture readings. At the end of the reflection, the leader continues by saying:

Leader   Let us reflect and pray in silence.

A period of silence is observed for private meditation, with or without music. Afterward, the leader continues the service — proceeding either to the Eucharistic Prayer or to the Prayers and Blessings after the optional hymn.

• In a small group, where all participants in the prayer service would be able to contribute if they wished, the leader should invite the community to share their personal reflections. This invitation may be devised by the prayer leader or use the following formula:

Leader   If you have any thoughts or prayers you would like to share, perhaps an image or a particular prayer from your prayers, please share them now as remembrances or prayerful desires for your companions. Please remember to be brief so everyone who desires will have an opportunity to speak.

The members of the community then share brief reflections or prayers. When appropriate, the leader ends these reflections by saying:

Leader   Let us reflect and pray in silence.

A period of silence is observed after the community members share their reflections, with or without music. Afterward, the leader continues the service — proceeding either to the Eucharistic Prayer or to the Prayers and Blessings after the optional hymn.

Hymn (optional)

Eucharistic Prayer

If the community wishes to share the Eucharist, the table is prepared during the hymn. If there is no hymn, the table should be prepared in silence — slowly and deliberately. Then, the leader begins the Eucharistic Prayer.

Leader   Thanks be to you, Holy Father of Glory,
father-kind, ever-loving, ever-powerful,
because of all the abundance, favor and deliverance
that you bestow on us in our need.

Community   **May your name be praised forever,
in the heavens above and here on earth.**

Leader   Whatever Providence befalls us as your children,
in our portion, in our lot, in our path,
give to us with it the riches of your hand
and the joyous blessing of your mouth.

Community   **May your kingdom be seen to flourish
through the joy of your people, always grateful.**

Leader   In the steep common path of our calling,
be it easy or uneasy to our flesh,
be it bright or dark for us to follow,
your perfect guidance will be upon us.

Community   **Provide for us in all our needs,
material and spiritual, this day and every day.**

Leader   Be a shield to us from the wiles of the deceiver,
from the arch-destroyer with his arrows pursuing us,
and in each secret thought our minds get to weave,
guide and protect us.

Community   **Do not allow us to be tossed about by temptations
and protect us from all evils that would do us harm.**

Leader   O Loving Christ, who was hanged upon a tree,
each day and each night we remember your covenant;
in our lying down and rising up, we yield ourselves to your cross,
in our lives and our deaths, we seek in you our peace.
Each day, may we remember the source of the mercies

16

bestowed on us, gently and generously;
each day, may we become fuller in love with you.

My brothers and sisters, with St. Paul, I say to you:

"I received from the Lord what I also handed on to you, that the Lord Jesus on the night when he was betrayed took a loaf of bread, and when he had given thanks, he broke it and said, 'This is my body that is for you. Do this in remembrance of me.' In the same way he took the cup also, after supper, saying, 'This cup is the new covenant in my blood. Do this, as often you drink it, in remembrance of me.' For as often as you eat this bread and drink the cup, you proclaim the Lord's death until he comes." (1 Corinthians 11: 23-26)

O Gracious God, *(making the sign of the cross)* your Spirit come upon us, and upon this bread and wine,

so that it might illumine our understanding, kindle our will, incite our love, strengthen our weakness, and enfold our desires.

Community	**O Generous Lord,**
	cleanse our hearts, make holy our souls, confirm our faith,
	keep safe our minds, encompass our bodies about,
	so that in our own hearts, we may feel your presence.
Leader	O Holy Spirit, of greatest power,
	come down upon us and subdue us;
	from your glorious mansion in the heavens.
	The knee that is stiff, O healer, make pliant,
	the heart that is cold, make warm beneath your wing;
	guide the soul that is wandering from your path and it shall not die.
	Each thing that is foul, may you cleanse,
	each thing that is hard, may you soften with your grace,
	each wound that is causing us pain, may you make whole.
	Now to the Father who created each creature,
	now to the Son who paid ransom for his people,
	now to the Holy Spirit, comforter of might:
	shield and protect us from every wound.

Community	**Encompass the beginning and the end of our race,**
	give us courage to sing in glory,
	in peace, in rest, in reconciliation.
Leader	Come share in the table of the Lord,
	source of love for those who cherish his kindness,
	source of solace for those who need his forgiveness,
	source of hope for those who fear his judgement.
	Come share in the table of the Lord.
Community	**Where no tear shall be shed,**
	where death comes no more. Amen.

The community shares the Eucharist in silence. Afterward, the table is cleared during the hymn. If there is no hymn, the members of the community use this time for private prayer.

Hymn (optional)

Then, the leader continues the service.

Prayers and Blessings

Leader	Praise to the Father,
	praise to the Son,
	praise to the Spirit.
Community	**The three in one.**

All stand. If necessary, the leader announces the version of the Lord's Prayer that will be used before continuing.

— The Lord's Prayer

Option A

Leader	Let us pray for the coming of the Kingdom,
	in the words our Lord taught us:
All	**"Our Father in heaven,**
	hallowed be your name.
	Your kingdom come.
	Your will be done,
	on earth as it is in heaven.

Give us this day our daily bread.
And forgive us our debts,
as we also have forgiven our debtors.
And do not bring us to the time of trial,
but rescue us from the evil one."
(Matthew 6: 9-13)

Leader   Thanks be to you, Eternal Father,
for you have enwrapped our bodies and our souls,
safeguarding us in the sanctuary of your love …

Community   **… and sheltering us under the mantle of your care.**
For the kingdom, the power, and the glory are yours
for ever and ever. Amen.

The leader should proceed to the Petition of Blessing beginning "O Holy God…" after Option B.

Option B

Leader   Let us pray for the coming of the Kingdom,
in the words our Lord taught us:

All   **Our Father in heaven,**
hallowed be your name,
your kingdom come,
your will be done,
on earth as in heaven.
Give us today our daily bread.
Forgive us our sins
as we forgive those who sin against us.
Lead us not into temptation
but deliver us from evil.

Leader   Thanks be to you, Eternal Father,
for you have enwrapped our bodies and our souls,
safeguarding us in the sanctuary of your love …

Community   **… and sheltering us under the mantle of your care.**
For the kingdom, the power, and the glory are yours
now and for ever.

— The Petition of Blessing

If necessary, the leader announces the Petition of Blessing selected for the prayer service before continuing.

Option A

Leader	O Holy God,
	guide us with your wisdom,
	chastise us with your justice,
	help us with your mercy,
	protect us with your strength.
	In our dreams…
Community	**… arouse holy ambitions.**
Leader	In our repose…
Community	**… strengthen us for your service.**
Leader	In our hearts…
Community	**… nurture love for all your creatures.**
Leader	In our minds…
Community	**… implant saintly thoughts.**
Leader	In our deeds…
Community	**… may others see your kindness.**
Leader	In our words…
Community	**… may others hear your mercy.**
Leader	In our wishes…
Community	**… may others feel your compassion.**
Leader	In our reason…
Community	**… may others discern your wisdom.**
Leader	Divine Majesty,
	fill us with your goodness,
	shield us with your shade,
	and change us with your grace.
Community	**Amen.**

The leader should proceed to the invitation to contemplate any private needs beginning "In the silence of your heart …" found after Option C.

Option B

Leader	O Holy God, we give you our whole soul:
	Our thoughts, our deeds, our words, our will,
	our understanding and our intellect.

	Everything we are sings your praises.
	We give you worship with our whole lives.
Community	**Keep us in the nearness of your love.**
Leader	We give you assent with our whole powers.
Community	**Keep us in the nearness of your love.**
Leader	We give you praise with our whole tongues.
Community	**Keep us in the nearness of your love.**
Leader	We give you honor with our whole utterances.
Community	**Keep us in the nearness of your love.**
Leader	We give you reverence with our whole understanding.
Community	**Keep us in the nearness of your love.**
Leader	We give you offering with our whole thoughts.
Community	**Keep us in the nearness of your love.**
Leader	We give you praise with our whole being.
Community	**Keep us in the nearness of your love.**
Leader	We give you love with our whole devotion.
Community	**Keep us in the nearness of your love.**
Leader	We give you kneeling with our whole desires.
Community	**Keep us in the nearness of your love.**
Leader	We give you love with our whole heart.
Community	**Keep us in the nearness of your love.**
Leader	We give you affection with our whole sense.
Community	**Keep us in the nearness of your love.**
Leader	We give you our existence with our whole mind.
Community	**Keep us in the nearness of your love.**
Leader	We beseech you, O God,
	keep us from all ill, hurt and harm,
	protect us from mischance, grief and despair,
	and guide us into the land of your peace.
Community	**Amen.**

The leader should proceed to the invitation to contemplate any private needs beginning "In the silence of your heart …" found after Option C.

Option C

Leader	O Holy God,
	give us of your wisdom,
	give us of your mercy,
	give us of your bounty,

	and guide us in the face of every challenge.
Community	**Help us to magnify the greatness of heaven,** **to magnify the greatness of God.**
Leader	Bless us and everything we touch, bless us in our every action.
Community	**Help us to magnify the greatness of heaven,** **to magnify the greatness of God.**
Leader	Protect us from every evil wish and sorrow, protect us and keep us safe while we live.
Community	**Help us to magnify the greatness of heaven,** **to magnify the greatness of God.**
Leader	Guide us as we travel the surface of the earth, guide us as we hope to return home.
Community	**Help us to magnify the greatness of heaven,** **to magnify the greatness of God.**
Leader	Assure us and make our faith grow in every day, assure us that we will reach your land of glory.
Community	**Help us to magnify the greatness of heaven,** **to magnify the greatness of God.**
Leader	Oh God, give us of your holiness, give us of your shielding, give us of your surrounding,
Community	**And bring us peace, in our lives and in our deaths.** **Amen.**

The leader continues.

Leader	In the silence of your heart, bring your special needs or concerns before God. If you wish us to join in your prayers for these needs, speak them aloud, saying when you are finished, "For this I pray."

Members of the community offer their particular prayers. The community's response to these individual petitions is:
> **May God's blessing be yours,**
> **and well may it befall you.**
When these personal prayers are finished, the leader offers the final blessings.

— The Final Blessing

If necessary, the leader announces the invocation selected for the prayer service before continuing.

Option A

Leader   May God our Father
be with you lying down,
be with you rising up.
May Christ our Brother
be with you sleeping,
be with you waking.
May the Spirit our Guide
be with you resting,
be with you acting.
May God the Father be with you, protecting;
May Christ our Lord be with you, directing;
may the Spirit of Grace be with you, strengthening;

Community   **For ever and for ever more. Amen.**

Proceed to the final blessing beginning "Praise to the Father ..." found after Option C.

Option B

Leader   May God our Creator
guard you from hurt and
protect you from harm
in the nearness of his love.
May Christ our Savior
shield you from mischance and
shelter you from grief
in the nearness of his love.
May the Guiding Spirit
keep you from ill and
bring you to the land of peace
in the nearness of his love.
Praise to the Father,

	praise to the Son, praise to the Spirit.
Community	**May the three in one bring us to the peace of eternity. Amen.**

Proceed to the final blessing beginning "Praise to the Father ..." found after Option C.

Option C

Leader	May the Father, Son and Spirit enfold you on every side, never forsaking or forgetting you, nor letting evil come near you, in each step of the journey before you. God the Father go with you at every pass, Christ our Lord be with you on every hill, The Spirit of Grace guide you across every stream. May the Triune God protect and keep you from every challenge and sorrow, from every evil and anguish,
Community	**Offering a mantle for both our bodies and our souls. Amen.**

The leader continues.

Leader	Praise to the Father, praise to the Son, praise to the Spirit.
Community	**The three in one.**
Leader	*(making the sign of the cross)* The guarding of the God of life be on you, the guarding of the loving Christ be on you, the guarding of the Holy Spirit be on you, aiding and enfolding you each day and night of your lives.
Community	**May God, the three in one, encompass us all, shielding us on sea and on land, in day and in night, guarding each step and each path we travel. Amen.**

Hymn (optional)

The members of the community may sit or kneel after the service concludes, as they prefer. Silence is observed to allow private prayer or meditation. Individuals should leave quietly as the Spirit moves them.

Petitions of Mercy

Option #1

Leader	Lord Jesus,
	keep the eye of God between us and every other eye;
	keep the purpose of God between us and every other purpose;
	keep the desire of God between us and every other desire;
	and no mouth can curse us.
	Lord Jesus, have mercy on us.
Community	**Lord Jesus, have mercy on us.**
Leader	Christ Jesus,
	keep your pain between us and every other pain;
	keep your love between us and every other love;
	keep your dearness between us and every other dearness;
	and no venom can wound us.
	Christ Jesus, have mercy on us.
Community	**Christ Jesus, have mercy on us.**
Leader	Lord Jesus,
	keep the desire of God between us and every other desire;
	keep the might of God between us and every other might;
	keep the right of God between us and every other right;
	and no ill thing can touch us.
	Lord Jesus, have mercy on us.
Community	**Lord Jesus, have mercy on us.**

Option #2

Leader	Lord Jesus,
	shielding us from harm,
	shielding us from ill,

	Lord Jesus, have mercy on us.
Community	**Lord Jesus, have mercy on us.**
Leader	Christ Jesus,
	shielding us from mishap,
	shielding us from danger,
	Christ Jesus, have mercy on us.
Community	**Christ Jesus, have mercy on us.**
Leader	Lord Jesus,
	shielding us with strength,
	shielding us with power,
	Lord Jesus, have mercy on us.
Community	**Lord Jesus, have mercy on us.**

Petitions of Blessing

Option #1

Leader	O Holy God, bless our homesteads and care for all therein. Help us also to remember those without home or refuge, especially those displaced by war and poverty.
Community	**May we all find refuge in the fellowship of Christ.**
Leader	O God, bless our kindred and protect those who are close to us. Help us also to remember those who are alone, without family or friends.
Community	**May we all find companionship in the fellowship of Christ.**
Leader	O God, bless our words and help them bring joy and comfort to others. Help us also to remember those who are harmed by unkind words and verbal abuse.
Community	**May we all hear the gentle voice welcoming us into the fellowship of Christ.**
Leader	O God, bless us in our errands and protect us in our travels. Help us also to remember those who are lost, walking through life without direction or hope.
Community	**May we all be guided into the fellowship of Christ.**
Leader	O God, lessen our sins and increase our trust in you. Help us also to remember those burdened by guilt and shame, especially those deep in despair.
Community	**May we all find forgiveness in the fellowship of Christ.**
Leader	O God, guard us from distress and protect us from misfortune. Help us also to remember those feeling battered by the turbulence of their lives, whether through their own choices or the actions of others.
Community	**May we all find consolation in the fellowship of Christ.**
Leader	O God, shelter us from harm and aid us in life's struggles, protect us under your shield and guard us from harm, guide us in your ways and clear the paths before us. Be by our knees, by our backs and by our sides in every step we take in this stormy world.

Community	**Amen.**

Option #2

Leader	O Holy God, be a smooth path before me, a guiding star above me, a keen eye behind me, this day, this night, forever. We are weary and forlorn,
Community	**Lead us to your house, to the peace of heaven.**
Leader	Help us do your will…
Community	**… and bridle our own.**
Leader	Help us give you your due…
Community	**… and put aside our entitlement.**
Leader	Help us travel your path…
Community	**… and leave behind our own.**
Leader	Help us ponder Christ's death…
Community	**… and find hope in our own.**
Leader	Help us meditate on Christ agony…
Community	**… and strengthen our love for you.**
Leader	Help us carry Christ's cross…
Community	**… and forget our own burdens.**
Leader	Help us embrace repentance…
Community	**… and accept your forgiveness.**
Leader	O Holy God, help us to bridle our tongues and our thoughts, so we may trust your wisdom, embrace Christ's redemptive love, and accept the Spirit's gentle graces. For we are weary and forlorn …
Community	**… and ask that you lead us to your house, to the peace of heaven. Amen.**

Final Blessings

Option #1

Leader	May the God of life encompass you,
	protecting your form and your frame.
	May the Christ of love encompass you,
	shielding you from hatred and from harm.
	May the spirit of grace encompass you,
	guiding you towards goodness and away from ill.
	The blessings of the Triune God surround you,
Community	**Abiding in us forever and eternally. Amen.**

Option #2

Leader	May the compassing of God the on you,
	the compassing of the God of life.
	May the compassing of Christ be on you,
	the compassing of the Christ of love.
	May the compassing of the Spirit be on you,
	the compassing of the Spirit of grace.
	May the compassing of the three be on you,
	the compassing of the three to preserve you.
Community	**The compassing of the three to preserve us. Amen.**

Prayer Sequences

The sequences may be used alone as discrete prayers in private devotion or in community worship. They also may be coordinated to the Carmichael Liturgy. With this in mind, it would be helpful to think about:

• Using These Prayers Alone

In each person's life, there are moments when they need something from God and these sequences are an opportunity to remember these desires. It is important to take some time to consider the particular needs that are being brought to these prayers and to find the sequence that best expresses these desires.

Also, take some time before using the sequences to reflect on the psalms and scriptural readings that will be used with them as well as any songs that might be incorporated into the coming prayer.

• Using These Prayers with Others

While the sequences are written in the first person, expressing personal needs in an intimate manner, they may be used with others so that individual voices come together in a shared expression of common needs. If using these sequences in a prayer group, one individual should serve as the leader and read the lines that are immediately at the margin and the rest of the community respond with those that are slightly indented, creating an antiphonal responsive reading.

In much the same way, it will be important before beginning the sequence to decide which member of the community will read the scriptural passages and how the group will read the psalm (i.e., at the same time or antiphonally).

• Using These Readings with the Carmichael Liturgy

As noted in the general introduction to this prayerbook, these sequences may be used to complement the use of the Carmichael Liturgy. If a community conducts the Carmichael Liturgy on a weekly basis, for example, the sequences may be used in the interval to focus individual or small group prayer. In much the same way, if the community conducts the Carmichael Liturgy on a daily basis (perhaps using the Eucharistic Prayer on one day of the week), then individuals may choose to use these sequences for private devotions addressing issues not expressed in the larger prayer service.

These prayer sequences should be spoken when used by groups for common worship, but individuals should decide whether they prefer to read the sequences aloud, to read them in silence or to read portions aloud (e.g., the scriptural selection, the psalm, the Lord's Prayer, etc.) to create a contrast between the different prayers. However the sequences are approached, it will be important to decide how to proceed when:

• Selecting Scriptural Readings

As with the Carmichael Liturgy, the readings used during the sequences may be selected to address a particular theme or to participate in the cycle of readings of a larger church community. Suggestions concerning the use of scriptural readings and psalms in these prayer sequences may be found in "Selecting Readings for the Liturgy and Sequences" in the Resources Section of this prayerbook.

• Including Songs and Hymns

If these sequences are being used for community prayer, the group may want to sing hymns during them. On the other hand, if the sequences are being used for private devotions, the individual may wish to listen to a recorded version of a favorite hymn or song. Suggestions concerning the use of scriptural readings and psalms in these prayer sequences may be found in "Using Music with the Liturgy and Sequences" in the Resources Section of this prayerbook.

• Giving Room for Silent Listening

These sequences are designed to help individuals and groups encounter God during the expression of their particular needs and concerns. So, it is important to make space during prayer to allow God to speak of his own hopes and desires for his creatures. With this in mind, do not rush through these prayers. Take time to read them slowly, perhaps taking a breath between sections of the sequences found on the margin and those that indented or pausing briefly when a space is found between the sections of the sequences.

Come I This Day

---

a morning prayer

*Quiet your spirit, becoming completely present to this moment.
Allow all other thoughts and concerns to fall away as you come into
the presence of God. Then, when you are ready, begin.*

Come I this day to the Father,
come I this day to the Son,
come I this day to the Holy Spirit powerful,
     come I this day with God,
     come I this day with Christ,
     come I with the Spirit of kindly balm.
God, and Spirit, and Jesus,
from the crown of my head
to the soles of my feet;
     come I with my reputation,
     come I with my testimony,
     come I to you, shelter me.

A Hymn, sung or heard (optional)

Thanks be to you, O Triune God,
who brought me from yesterday
to the beginning of today,
     for every gift of peace you bestow on me.
My thoughts, my words,
my deeds, my desires
     I dedicate to you.
I beseech you,
to keep me from offense,
     and to shield me with the offering of your grace.
Bless to me, O God,
     my soul and my body;
bless to me, O God,
     my belief and my condition;
bless to me, O God,
     my heart and my speech,
and bless to me, O God,

the handling of my hand.
O God, enfold me,
        O God, surround me!
Be in my speaking,
        be in my thinking,
be in my sleeping,
        be in my waking,
be in my watching,
        be in my hoping.
Be in my life,
        be in my lips,
be in my hands,
        be in my heart,
        till I go to sleep this night.

A Psalm, read or recited

O God,
Father, Son and Spirit,
guide me with your wisdom,
        chastise me with your justice,
help me with your mercy,
        protect me with your strength.

A Scriptural Reading, read aloud or quietly

O God,
Father, Son and Spirit,
fill me with your fullness,
        shield me with your shade,
fill me with your grace,
        for the sake of your love everlasting.

O God,
Father, Son and Spirit,
who brought me from the rest of last night
unto the joyous light of this day,
bring me from the new light of this day
unto the guiding light of eternity.
Give to me, O God,

each food that is needful for my body,
give to me, O God,
each light that is needful for my mind,
give to me, O God,
each salve that is needful for my soul.
give to me, O God,
sincere repentance;
give to me, O God,
whole-hearted repentance;
give to me, O God,
lasting repentance.
Give to me, O God,
to confess the death of Christ;
give to me, O God,
to meditate the agony of Christ;
give to me, O God,
to make warm the love of Christ.
O great God of Heaven,
draw my soul to yourself,
that I may make repentance
with the right and strong heart,
with a heart broken and contrite.

O God,
Father, Son and Spirit,
be with me on this your day,
Amen.
Anything that is evil to me,
or that may witness against me
where I shall longest be,
illume it to me,
banish it from me,
root it out of my heart,
ever, ever more, everlastingly.

Select one of the following options for the Lord's Prayer.

Option A

O God,

Father, Son and Spirit,
help me pray as Jesus himself taught:
> "Our Father in heaven,
> hallowed be your name.
> Your kingdom come.
> Your will be done,
> on earth as it is in heaven.
> Give us this day our daily bread.
> And forgive us our debts,
> as we also have forgiven our debtors.
> And do not bring us to the time of trial,
> but rescue us from the evil one."
> (Matthew 6: 9-13)

Thanks be to you, Eternal Father,
for you have enwrapped my body and my soul,
safeguarding me in the sanctuary of your love
and sheltering me under the mantle of your care.
> For the kingdom, and the power, and the glory,
> are yours for ever and ever. Amen.

Please proceed with "The peace of the Father of joy...," found after Option B.

Option B

O God,
Father, Son and Spirit,
help me pray as Jesus himself taught:
> Our Father in heaven,
> hallowed be your name,
> your kingdom come,
> your will be done,
> on earth as in heaven.
> Give us today our daily bread.
> Forgive us our sins
> as we forgive those who sin against us.
> Lead us not into temptation
> but deliver us from evil.

Thanks be to you, Eternal Father,
for you have enwrapped my body and my soul,

safeguarding me in the sanctuary of your love
and sheltering me under the mantle of your care.
>For the kingdom, the power, and the glory
>are yours now and for ever.

The peace of the Father of joy,
the peace of the Christ of tenderness,
the peace of the Spirit of grace,
be upon each thing my eye takes in,
upon my body that is of earth
and upon my soul it came from on high,
>upon my body that is of earth
>and upon my soul that came from on high.
Bless, O holy Trinity, my face,
let my face bless everything;
>bless, O holy Trinity, my eye,
>let my eye bless all it sees.
The peace of the Father be to me,
the peace of Christ be to me,
the peace of the Spirit be to me,
during all my life,
during all the days of my life.
>The peace of God be to all,
>the peace of Christ be to all,
>the peace of the Spirit be to all,
>during all their lives,
>during all the days of their lives.

A Hymn, sung or heard (optional)

The Father be with me in every pass,
Jesus be with me on every hill,
the Spirit be with me on every stream,
headland and ridge and lawn.
>Thanks be to you, O God,
>Father, Son and Spirit,
>that I have risen today,
>to the rising of this life itself;
>may it be to your own glory, O God of every gift,
>and to the glory of my soul likewise.

End this time of prayer by taking some time to bring to mind the gifts God will give you in the coming day and resolve to use these gifts wisely and well. Then, when you are ready, conclude by saying:

I am bending my knee
in the eye of the Father who created me,
in the eye of the Son who purchased me,
in the eye of the Spirit who cleansed me,
in friendship and affection. Amen.

I Lie Down This Night With God

a night prayer

> *Quiet your spirit, becoming completely present to this moment.*
> *Allow all other thoughts and concerns to fall away as you come into*
> *the presence of God. Then, when you are ready, begin.*

I lie down this night with God,
     and God will lie down with me;
I lie down this night with Christ,
     and Christ will lie down with me;
I lie down this night with the Spirit,
     and the Spirit will lie down with me;
God and Christ and the Spirit
     be lying down with me.
I am placing my soul and my body
in your sanctuary this night, O Father,
in your sanctuary, O Jesus Christ,
in your sanctuary, O Spirit of perfect truth;
     The Three will defend my cause,
     never turning their backs upon me.

A Hymn, sung or heard (optional)

O Triune God of Life,
I am placing my soul and my body
     under your guarding this night, O loving Father.
I am placing my soul and my body
     under your guarding this night, O caring Lord.
I am placing my soul and my body
     under your guarding this night, O guiding Spirit.
O God of Life,
shield and sustain me this night,
     this night and every night.
guard me in my body, guard me in my soul;
     guard me this night in my body and my soul.
guard me in my life, guard me in my creed,
     guard me and my tie to my life and to my creed.
guard me in my speech, guard me in my heart;

guard me in every whit in my speech and in my heart.
O God of Life,
bless to me the moon that is above me,
     bless to me the earth that is beneath me,
bless to me those you have given me to love,
     and bless to me, O God, myself who have care of them.
Bless to me the things on which my eyes rest,
     bless to me the things on which my hopes rest,
bless to me my reason and my purpose.
     Bless all these things, O God of life.
O God of Life,
darken not to me your light,
     close not to me your joy,
shut not to me your door
     and refuse not to me your mercy.
     O God, crown me with your gladness!

A Psalm, read or recited

O God,
Father, Son and Spirit
guide me with your wisdom,
     chastise me with your justice,
help me with your mercy,
     protect me with your strength.

A Scriptural Reading, read aloud or quietly

O God,
Father, Son and Spirit
fill me with your fullness,
     shield me with your shade,
fill me with your grace,
     for the sake of your love everlasting.

O God,
Father, Son and Spirit,
Shield and sustain me this night,
     this night and every night.
Grant that the shielding of the Spirit be mine this night,

grant that the shielding of the Son be mine this night,
grant that the shielding of the Father be mine this night.
Grant that this shielding be mine this night,
from my lying down at dusk to my rising at day.
Grant that the sustaining of the Spirit be mine this night,
grant that the sustaining of the Son be mine this night,
grant that the sustaining of the Father be mine this night.
Grant that this sustaining be mine this night,
from my lying down at dusk to my rising at day.
Grant that the peace of the Spirit be mine this night,
grant that the peace of the Son be mine this night,
grant that the peace of the Father be mine this night.
Grant that this peace be mine this night,
from my lying down at dusk to my rising at day.
O Holy Triune God,
Pour down upon me from heaven
the rich blessing of your forgiveness.
Grant to me, the fear of you, the love of you,
and the will to do on earth at all times
as angels and saints do in heaven.
In trust and love, I am giving to you this night
all my mind, all my will, and all my hope;
I am giving to you this night
my soul everlasting and my body;
And fervently I pray your strong protection
from my lying down at dusk to my rising at day.

O God,
Father, Son and Spirit
be with me on this your night,
Amen.
Anything that is evil to me,
or that may witness against me
where I shall longest be,
illume it to me,
banish it from me,
root it out of my heart,
ever, ever more, everlastingly.

Select one of the following options for the Lord's Prayer.

Option A

O God,
Father, Son and Spirit,
help me pray as Jesus himself taught:
> "Our Father in heaven,
> hallowed be your name.
> Your kingdom come.
> Your will be done,
> on earth as it is in heaven.
> Give us this day our daily bread.
> And forgive us our debts,
> as we also have forgiven our debtors.
> And do not bring us to the time of trial,
> but rescue us from the evil one."
> (Matthew 6: 9-13)

Thanks be to you, Eternal Father,
for you have enwrapped my body and my soul,
safeguarding me in the sanctuary of your love
and sheltering me under the mantle of your care.
> For the kingdom, and the power, and the glory,
> are yours for ever and ever. Amen.

Please proceed with "The peace of the Father of joy...," found after Option B.

Option B

O God,
Father, Son and Spirit,
help me pray as Jesus himself taught:
> Our Father in heaven,
> hallowed be your name,
> your kingdom come,
> your will be done,
> on earth as in heaven.
> Give us today our daily bread.
> Forgive us our sins
> as we forgive those who sin against us.

Lead us not into temptation
but deliver us from evil.
Thanks be to you, Eternal Father,
for you have enwrapped my body and my soul,
safeguarding me in the sanctuary of your love
and sheltering me under the mantle of your care.
For the kingdom, the power, and the glory
are yours now and for ever.

The peace of the Father of joy,
the peace of the Christ of tenderness,
the peace of the Spirit of grace,
be upon each thing my eye takes in,
upon my body that is of earth
and upon my soul that came from on high,
upon my body that is of earth
and upon my soul that came from on high.
Bless, O holy Trinity, my face,
let my face bless everything;
bless, O holy Trinity, my eye,
let my eye bless all it sees.
The peace of God be to me,
the peace of Christ be to me,
the peace of the Spirit be to me,
during all my life,
during all the days of my life.
The peace of the Father be to all,
the peace of Christ be to all,
the peace of the Spirit be to all,
during all their lives,
during all the days of their lives.

A Hymn, sung or heard (optional)

O Father, kind and just,
O Son, who did overcome death,
O Holy Spirit of power,
Be keeping me this night from harm;
The Three who would justify me
Keeping me this night and always.

I am beseeching you
to keep me from ill,
to keep me from harm,
to keep me from mischance,
to keep me from grief,
to keep me this night
in the nearness of your love.

End this time of prayer by taking some time to bring to mind the gifts God gave you in the passing day — as well as the protection offered during the coming night — and resolve to use these gifts wisely and well. Then, when you are ready, conclude by saying:

I am bending my knee
in the eye of the Father who created me,
in the eye of the Son who purchased me,
in the eye of the Spirit who cleansed me,
in friendship and affection. Amen.

for protection of body and soul in troubled times

> *Quiet your spirit, becoming completely present to this moment. Allow all other thoughts and concerns to fall away as you come into the presence of God. Then, when you are ready, begin.*

I am praying and appealing to the Father,
the Son of Mary and the Spirit of truth,
to aid me in distress of sea and of land:
      may the Three succor me, may the Three shield me,
      may the Three watch me by day and by night.
Father and Jesus and the Spirit of cleansing
be shielding me, be possessing me, be aiding me,
be clearing my path and going before my soul
      in hollow, on hill, on plain,
      on sea and land be the Three aiding me.

A Hymn, sung or heard (optional)

O Holy God,
Father and Jesus and the Holy Spirit,
be shielding and saving me,
      as Three and as One,
Shield me from the grudge of ill-wishers
      and snatch me from the snares of spiteful ones;
succor me and shield me with your linen mantle
      and draw me to the shelter house of the saintly.
Keep me from all malice, from every angry barb;
      keep me from all spite, from evil and anguish.
Grant that I shall not be left in the hands of the wicked,
Grant that I shall not be bent in the court of the false,
      Grant that I shall rise victorious above them
      as rise victorious the arches of the waves.
O Holy God,
Father and Jesus and the Holy Spirit,
I am placing my soul and my body under your guarding.
Bless to me the land whither I am bound,
      bless the things my eyes shall see,

bless to me the thing my purpose discerns,
O God of life, bless and guard my condition.
Bless the journey whereon I go,
bless the earth that is under my foot,
bless the matter which I see,
O King of Glory, bless and guard my condition.
O Holy God,
Father and Jesus and the Holy Spirit,
remember me always and shield me under your wing;
do not forsake me, O Rock of Truth,
for my need it is ever to be near you.

A Psalm, read or recited

O God,
Father, Son and Spirit
guide me with your wisdom,
chastise me with your justice,
help me with your mercy,
protect me with your strength.

A Scriptural Reading, read aloud or quietly

O God,
Father, Son and Spirit
fill me with your fullness,
shield me with your shade,
fill me with your grace,
for the sake of your love everlasting.

O God,
Father, Son and Spirit
be at my breast, be at my back,
be to me as a star, be to me as a guide,
from my life's beginning to its closing.
Be between me and all things grizzly,
be between me and all things mean,
be between me and all things gruesome
coming darkly towards me.
Encompass me, O Everlasting Father of Life,

encompass me, O Son of God and of Mary,
encompass me, O Mild Shepherding Spirit.
       encompass me, as Three and as One,
Be always before me,
       be always behind me,
be always over me,
       be always under me,
be laws with me,
       be always around me.
O God of Power, shield and sustain me!
       Succor and guard me under your wing!
Give me of your wisdom,
       give me of your mercy,
give me of your holiness,
       and give me of your guidance
       in the face of every strait.
Aid my steps, O Holy Trinity,
leading me to the life eternal
       in the paradise of the godly,
       in the sun-garden of your love.

O God,
Father, Son and Spirit,
be with me on this your day,
       Amen.
Be with me on this your night,
       Amen.
Anything that is evil to me,
or that may witness against me
where I shall longest be,
       illume it to me,
       banish it from me,
       root it out of my heart,
       ever, ever more, everlastingly.

Select one of the following options for the Lord's Prayer.

Option A

O God,

Father, Son and Spirit,
help me pray as Jesus himself taught:
> "Our Father in heaven,
> hallowed be your name.
> Your kingdom come.
> Your will be done,
> on earth as it is in heaven.
> Give us this day our daily bread.
> And forgive us our debts,
> as we also have forgiven our debtors.
> And do not bring us to the time of trial,
> but rescue us from the evil one."
> (Matthew 6: 9-13)

Thanks be to you, Eternal Father,
for you have enwrapped my body and my soul,
safeguarding me in the sanctuary of your love
and sheltering me under the mantle of your care.
> For the kingdom, and the power, and the glory,
> are yours for ever and ever. Amen.

Please proceed with "The peace of the Father of joy...," found after Option B.

Option B

O God,
Father, Son and Spirit,
help me pray as Jesus himself taught:
> Our Father in heaven,
> hallowed be your name,
> your kingdom come,
> your will be done,
> on earth as in heaven.
> Give us today our daily bread.
> Forgive us our sins
> as we forgive those who sin against us.
> Lead us not into temptation
> but deliver us from evil.

Thanks be to you, Eternal Father,
for you have enwrapped my body and my soul,

safeguarding me in the sanctuary of your love
and sheltering me under the mantle of your care.
>For the kingdom, the power, and the glory
>are yours now and for ever.

The peace of the Father of joy,
the peace of the Christ of tenderness,
the peace of the Spirit of grace,
be upon each thing my eye takes in,
upon my body that is of earth
and upon my soul that came from on high,
>upon my body that is of earth
>and upon my soul that came from on high.
Bless, O holy Trinity, my face,
let my face bless everything;
>bless, O holy Trinity, my eye,
>let my eye bless all it sees.
The peace of the Father be to me,
the peace of Christ be to me,
the peace of the Spirit be to me,
during all my life,
during all the days of my life.
>The peace of God be to all,
>the peace of Christ be to all,
>the peace of the Spirit be to all,
>during all their lives,
>during all the days of their lives.

A Hymn, sung or heard (optional)

O God, my soul's healer,
keep me at even,
keep me at morning,
keep me at noon,
on rough coarse fairing,
help and safeguard
my means this night.
>I am tired, astray, and stumbling,
>shield me from snare and sin.
>God and Jesus and the Holy Spirit

Be shielding and saving me,
As Three and as One,
By my knee, by my back, by my side,
Each step of the stormy world.

End this time of prayer by taking some time to bring to mind the various ways God shields you from harm or guides you through the world's tumult. Then, when you are ready, conclude by saying:

I am bending my knee
in the eye of the Father who created me,
in the eye of the Son who purchased me,
in the eye of the Spirit who cleansed me,
in friendship and affection. Amen.

Bless To Me, O Christ, The Path Whereon I Go

for confidence to share Christ's love with others

> *Quiet your spirit, becoming completely present to this moment. Allow all other thoughts and concerns to fall away as you come into the presence of God. Then, when you are ready, begin.*

Bless to me, O Lord Jesus,
the earth beneath my foot,
bless to me, O Christ,
the path whereon I go;
> bless to me, O Lord Jesus,
> the thing of my desire;
> thou evermore of evermore,
> bless to me my rest.
Bless to me the thing
whereon is set my mind,
bless to me the thing
whereon is set my love;
> bless to me the thing
> whereon is set my hope;
> O King of Kings,
> bless to me my eye!

A Hymn, sung or heard (optional)

Thanks be to you, Jesus Christ,
for the many gifts you have bestowed on me,
> each day and night, each sea and land,
> each weather fair, each calm, each wild.
O son of God, be shielding me from harm,
> O son of God, be shielding me from ill,
O son of God, be shielding me from mishap,
> O son of God, be shielding me this night.
O son of God, be guarding me with might,
> O son of God, be guarding me with power.
O son of God, be freeing me from every wickedness,
> O son of God, be freeing me from every entrapment,
O son of God, be freeing me from every gully,

O son of God, be freeing me from every torturous road.
O son of God, be opening to me every pass,
      O son of God, be opening to me every narrow way,
To whom shall I offer oblation?
      Because of all that I have seen,
      of your peace and of your mercy,
      I lift my soul to you, O Lord of all lords.
I am giving you praise with my whole tongue,
      I am giving you honor with my whole utterance.
I am giving you reverence with my whole understanding,
      I am giving you offering with my whole thought,
I am giving you my existence with my whole mind,
      I am giving you my soul, O God of all gods.
I am beseeching you to keep me from ill,
      to keep me from harm,
to keep me from mischance,
      to keep me from grief,
to keep me always in the nearness of your love.
      To keep me always in the nearness of your love.

A Psalm, read or recited

O Lord, Lamb of God,
son of God and son of Mary,
guide me with your wisdom,
      chastise me with your justice,
help me with your mercy,
      protect me with your strength.

A Scriptural Reading, read aloud or quietly

O Lord, Lamb of God,
son of God and son of Mary,
fill me with your fullness,
      shield me with your shade,
fill me with your grace,
      for the sake of your love everlasting.

O Lord, Lamb of God,
son of God and son of Mary,

May you be at the outset of my journey,
      may you be in surety to aid me;
may you make clear my way,
      may you be at the end of my seeking.
O Christ, enfold me
      and surround me.
O Christ, be always in my speaking,
      and be always in my thinking,
O Christ, be always in my watching,
      and be always in my hoping,
O Christ, be always in my lips,
      and be always in my hands,
O Christ, be always in my heart.
      and be always in my ever-living soul.
O Holy Lord, strengthen me in every good
      and encompass me in every strait,
safeguard me in every ill
      and from every enmity restrain me.
O Holy Lord, may my life magnify the greatness of heaven,
      so that my life may magnify the love of God,
may my life magnify your own greatness,
      so that my life may magnify your own love.
The love and shelter that you give to me
      grant that I may give to whoever meets me.
The peace and joy that you give to me
      grant that I may give to whoever meets me.
I say this prayer from my mouth, O Son of the God of Grace
      I say this prayer from my heart, O Son of the God of Grace.

O Lord, Lamb of God,
son of God and son of Mary,
be with me on this your day,
      Amen.
Be with me on this your night,
      Amen.
Anything that is evil to me,
or that may witness against me
where I shall longest be,
      illume it to me,
      banish it from me,

root it out of my heart,
ever, ever more, everlastingly.

Select one of the following options for the Lord's Prayer.

Option A

O Lord, Lamb of God,
son of God and son of Mary,
help me pray as you yourself taught:
       "Our Father in heaven,
       hallowed be your name.
       Your kingdom come.
       Your will be done,
       on earth as it is in heaven.
       Give us this day our daily bread.
       And forgive us our debts,
       as we also have forgiven our debtors.
       And do not bring us to the time of trial,
       but rescue us from the evil one."
       (Matthew 6: 9-13)
Thanks be to my Eternal Father,
who has enwrapped my body and my soul,
       safeguarding me in the sanctuary of his love
       and sheltering me under the mantle of his care.
Thanks be to you, Eternal Father,
       For the kingdom, and the power, and the glory,
       are yours for ever and ever. Amen.

Please proceed with "The peace of Christ, the Lamb of God...," found after Option B.

Option B

O Lord, Lamb of God,
son of God and son of Mary,
help me pray as you yourself taught:
       Our Father in heaven,
       hallowed be your name,
       your kingdom come,

your will be done,
on earth as in heaven.
Give us today our daily bread.
Forgive us our sins
as we forgive those who sin against us.
Lead us not into temptation
but deliver us from evil.
Thanks be to my Eternal Father,
who has enwrapped my body and my soul,
safeguarding me in the sanctuary of his love
and sheltering me under the mantle of his care.
Thanks be to you, Eternal Father,
For the kingdom, and the power, and the glory,
are yours for ever and ever. Amen.

The peace of Christ, the Lamb of God,
be upon each thing my eye takes in,
upon my body that is of earth
and upon my soul that came from on high,
upon my body that is of earth
and upon my soul that came from on high.
Bless, O holy Lord, my face,
let my face bless everything;
bless, O holy Lord, my eye,
let my eye bless all it sees.
The peace of Christ be to me,
during all my life,
during all the days of my life.
The peace of Christ be to to all,
during all their lives,
during all the days of their lives.

A Hymn, sung or heard (optional)

May I speak each day according to your justice,
each day may I show your chastening, O Christ;
May I speak each day according to your wisdom,
each day and night may I be at peace with you.
May I each day give love to you, O Jesus,
each night may I do the same;

each day and night, dark and light,
May I laud your goodness to me, O Lord.

End this time of prayer by taking some time to bring to mind the many ways God strengthens and supports your desire to be an instrument of the Divine Presence and resolve to trust in these gifts as you face the challenges in your life. Then, when you are ready, conclude by saying:

I am bending my knee
in the eye of the Father who created me,
in the eye of the Son who purchased me,
in the eye of the Spirit who cleansed me,
in friendship and affection. Amen.

Lift From Me, O God, My Anguish

for consolation in times of distress or pain

Quiet your spirit, becoming completely present to this moment. Allow all other thoughts and concerns to fall away as you come into the presence of God. Then, when you are ready, begin.

O great God, grant me your light,
O great God, grant me your grace,
O great God, grant me your joy,
      and let me be made pure in the well of your health.
Lift from me, O God, my anguish,
lift from me, O God, my abhorrence,
lift from me, O God, all empty pride,
      and lighten my soul in the light of your love.

A Hymn, sung or heard (optional)

O Holy Triune God,
hearken to my prayer,
let my earnest petition come to you,
      for I know that you are hearing me
      as surely as if I saw you with my eyes.
I am weary, weak and cold,
I am weary, troubled of soul,
      I am weary, racked by anguish,
      I am weary, crippled by pain
O Holy Trinity, accept the caring for my tears
and grant me peace in the nearness of your repose.
      All that is amiss for my mind or body,
      All that is amiss for my soul,
      for this life or the next,
O Holy Trinity, sweep it from me
      and shield me in the mantle of your love.
Let no thought come to my heart,
let no sound come to my ear,
      let no temptation come to my mind,
      let no trouble come to my spirit,
that is hurtful to my poor body in this life,

nor ill for my soul at the hour of my death;
O Loving God, bright and kindly,
I beseech you with earnestness,
    I beseech you with humbleness,
I beseech you with lowliness,
    I beseech you with tearfulness,
I beseech you with kneeling,
    that I might find rest everlasting
    in the repose of the Trinity,
    in the paradise of the godly,
    in the vine-garden of your love.

A Psalm, read or recited

O God,
Father, Son and Spirit
guide me with your wisdom,
    chastise me with your justice,
help me with your mercy,
    protect me with your strength.

A Scriptural Reading, read aloud or quietly

O God,
Father, Son and Spirit
fill me with your fullness,
    shield me with your shade,
fill me with your grace,
    for the sake of your love everlasting.

O God,
Father, Son and Spirit,
I am here in need,
I am here in pain,
I am here alone.
O Holy Trinity, aid me!
Grant unto me your light,
grant unto me your grace,
grant unto me your joy
    and let me be made pure in the well of your health.

Lift out from me my anguish,
lift out from me my abhorrence,
lift out from me my all-empty pride
and lighten my soul in the light of your love.
O God of life, darken not to me your light,
O God of life, close not to me your joy,
O God of life, shut not to me your door,
O God of life, refuse not to me your mercy,
Give instead each food that is needful for my body,
each light that is needful for my mind
and each salve that is needful for my soul.
O Great God of Heaven,
draw my soul to yourself
and bring me to the dwelling of peace.
As I put off from me my raiment,
grant me to put off my struggling;
as the haze rises from the crest of the mountains,
you raise my soul from the vapor of death.
O Great God of Heaven,
guard my body and my mind in the shielding of your mantle
and make clean my soul in the purifying of your grace.

O God,
Father, Son and Spirit,
be with me on this your day,
Amen.
Be with me on this your night,
Amen.
Anything that is evil to me,
or that may witness against me
where I shall longest be,
illume it to me,
banish it from me,
root it out of my heart,
ever, ever more, everlastingly.

Select one of the following options for the Lord's Prayer.

Option A

O God,
Father, Son and Spirit,
help me pray as Jesus himself taught:
> "Our Father in heaven,
> hallowed be your name.
> Your kingdom come.
> Your will be done,
> on earth as it is in heaven.
> Give us this day our daily bread.
> And forgive us our debts,
> as we also have forgiven our debtors.
> And do not bring us to the time of trial,
> but rescue us from the evil one."
> (Matthew 6: 9-13)

Thanks be to you, Eternal Father,
for you have enwrapped my body and my soul,
safeguarding me in the sanctuary of your love
and sheltering me under the mantle of your care.
> For the kingdom, and the power, and the glory,
> are yours for ever and ever. Amen.

Please proceed with "The peace of the Father of joy...," found after Option B.

Option B

O God,
Father, Son and Spirit,
help me pray as Jesus himself taught:
> Our Father in heaven,
> hallowed be your name,
> your kingdom come,
> your will be done,
> on earth as in heaven.
> Give us today our daily bread.
> Forgive us our sins
> as we forgive those who sin against us.
> Lead us not into temptation
> but deliver us from evil.

Thanks be to you, Eternal Father,

for you have enwrapped my body and my soul,
safeguarding me in the sanctuary of your love
and sheltering me under the mantle of your care.
> For the kingdom, the power, and the glory
> are yours now and for ever.

The peace of the Father of joy,
the peace of the Christ of tenderness,
the peace of the Spirit of grace,
be upon each thing my eye takes in,
upon my body that is of earth
and upon my soul that came from on high,
> upon my body that is of earth
> and upon my soul that came from on high.

Bless, O holy Trinity, my face,
let my face bless everything;
> bless, O holy Trinity, my eye,
> let my eye bless all it sees.

The peace of the Father be to me,
the peace of Christ be to me,
the peace of the Spirit be to me,
during all my life,
during all the days of my life.
> The peace of God be to all,
> the peace of Christ be to all,
> the peace of the Spirit be to all,
> during all their lives,
> during all the days of their lives.

A Hymn, sung or heard (optional)

O God of life, darken not to me your light,
O God of life, close not to me your joy,
O God of life, shut not to me your door,
O God of life, refuse not to me your mercy,
> As I put off from me my raiment,
> Grant me to put off my struggling;
> As the haze rises from the crest of the mountains,
> You raise my soul from the vapor of death.

End this time of prayer by taking some time to bring to mind the ways God consoles you when you are frightened or in pain. Also, contemplate the many ways God heals the wounds of your suffering. Then, when you are ready, conclude by saying:

I am bending my knee
in the eye of the Father who created me,
in the eye of the Son who purchased me,
in the eye of the Spirit who cleansed me,
in friendship and affection. Amen.

O Great God, Aid My Soul

---

for the continuing guidance of God's presence

Quiet your spirit, becoming completely present to this moment. Allow all other thoughts and concerns to fall away as you come into the presence of God. Then, when you are ready, begin.

O Holy Triune God, aid my soul
with the aiding of your own mercy;
  even as I clothe my body with wool,
  cover my soul with the shadow of your wing.
Help me to avoid every sin,
and the source of every sin to forsake;
  and as the mist scatters on the crest of the hills,
  may each ill haze clear from my soul, O God.

A Hymn, sung or heard (optional)

Holy Triune God,
bless the pathway on which I go,
bless the earth that is beneath my sole;
  bless all, O God, and give to me your love,
O Father, beloved of every naked one,
from whom all gifts and goodness come,
my heart illumine with your mercy,
  in your mercy shield me from all harm.
O King of kings, Lord of lords,
without your divinity there is nothing
in man that can earn esteem;
  without you, sinless man can never be.
O Holy Spirit of greatest power,
come down upon me and subdue me;
from your glorious mansion in the heavens,
  your radiant light shed on me.
Nourishment are you, of all things the best
against the soul of wildest speech;
  food are you, sweeter than all;
  sustain and guide your creatures at every time.
The knee that is stiff make pliant,

the heart that is hard make warm beneath your wing;
  the soul that is wandering from your path,
  grasp you its helm and it shall not die.
Each thing that is foul you cleanse early,
each thing that is hard you soften with your grace,
  each wound that is causing pain,
  O best of healers, make you whole!
O Holy God,
Give to me the grace to be diligent
  and to put my trust wholly in you.

A Psalm, read or recited

O God,
Father, Son and Spirit
guide me with your wisdom,
  chastise me with your justice,
help me with your mercy,
  protect me with your strength.

A Scriptural Reading, read aloud or quietly

O God,
Father, Son and Spirit
fill me with your fullness,
  shield me with your shade,
fill me with your grace,
  for the sake of your love everlasting.

O God,
Father, Son and Spirit,
be with me in every pass,
be with me on every hill,
  be with me on every stream,
  headland and ridge and lawn;
Each sea and land, each moor and meadow,
each lying down, each rising up,
  in the trough of the waves, on the crest of the billows,
  in each step of the paths I travel.
O Holy Triune God,

who brought me from the rest of last night
unto the joyous light of this day,
        be bringing me from the new light of this day
        unto the guiding light of eternity.
Each day may I remember the source of the mercies
you have bestowed on me gently and generously;
        each day may I be fuller in love to yourself.
Each thing I have received, from you it came,
        each thing for which I hope, from your love it will come,
each thing I enjoy, it is of your bounty,
        each thing I asked, comes of your disposing.
Grant me to have this living prayer:
lighten my understanding, kindle my will, begin my doing,
incite my love, strengthen my weakness, enfold my desire.
        Cleanse my heart, make holy my soul, confirm my faith,
        keep safe my mind and compass my body about.
As I utter my prayer from my mouth,
        in my own heart may I feel your presence.

O God,
Father, Son and Spirit,
be with me on this your day,
        Amen.
Be with me on this your night,
        Amen.
Anything that is evil to me,
or that may witness against me
where I shall longest be,
        illume it to me,
        banish it from me,
        root it out of my heart,
        ever, ever more, everlastingly.

Select one of the following options for the Lord's Prayer.

Option A

O God,
Father, Son and Spirit,
help me pray as Jesus himself taught:

"Our Father in heaven,
hallowed be your name.
Your kingdom come.
Your will be done,
on earth as it is in heaven.
Give us this day our daily bread.
And forgive us our debts,
as we also have forgiven our debtors.
And do not bring us to the time of trial,
but rescue us from the evil one."
(Matthew 6: 9-13)
Thanks be to you, Eternal Father,
for you have enwrapped my body and my soul,
safeguarding me in the sanctuary of your love
and sheltering me under the mantle of your care.
For the kingdom, and the power, and the glory,
are yours for ever and ever. Amen.

Please proceed with "The peace of the Father of joy…," found after Option B.

Option B

O God,
Father, Son and Spirit,
help me pray as Jesus himself taught:
Our Father in heaven,
hallowed be your name,
your kingdom come,
your will be done,
on earth as in heaven.
Give us today our daily bread.
Forgive us our sins
as we forgive those who sin against us.
Lead us not into temptation
but deliver us from evil.
Thanks be to you, Eternal Father,
for you have enwrapped my body and my soul,
safeguarding me in the sanctuary of your love
and sheltering me under the mantle of your care.

For the kingdom, the power, and the glory
are yours now and for ever.

The peace of the Father of joy,
the peace of the Christ of tenderness,
the peace of the Spirit of grace,
be upon each thing my eye takes in,
upon my body that is of earth
and upon my soul that came from on high,
      upon my body that is of earth
      and upon my soul that came from on high.
Bless, O holy Trinity, my face,
let my face bless everything;
      bless, O holy Trinity, my eye,
      let my eye bless all it sees.
The peace of the Father be to me,
the peace of Christ be to me,
the peace of the Spirit be to me,
during all my life,
during all the days of my life.
      The peace of God be to all,
      the peace of Christ be to all,
      the peace of the Spirit be to all,
      during all their lives,
      during all the days of their lives.

A Hymn, sung or heard (optional)

O Holy Triune God,
be a smooth way before me,
be a guiding star above me,
be a keen eye behind me,
this day, this night, for ever.
      O God of life,
      Father, Son and Spirit,
      be at peace with me, be my support,
      be to me as a star, be to me as a helm,
      from my waking until my sleeping,
      from my lying down in peace to my rising anew.

End this time of prayer by taking some time to bring to mind the many ways God guides you in your life and how you respond to that guidance. Ask for a discerning heart and the strength to follow the paths God sets before you. Then, when you are ready, conclude by saying:

I am bending my knee
in the eye of the Father who created me,
in the eye of the Son who purchased me,
in the eye of the Spirit who cleansed me,
in friendship and affection. Amen.

---

for the acceptance of God's forgiveness

*Quiet your spirit, becoming completely present to this moment.
Allow all other thoughts and concerns to fall away as you come into
the presence of God. Then, when you are ready, begin.*

Thanks be to you, Lord Jesus Christ,
Lamb of God and God of all Glory,
for all the abundance, favor, and deliverance
that you bestowed upon me in my need.
     I am guilty and polluted, O Lord,
     in spirit, in heart, and in flesh,
     in thought, in word, in act,
     I am hard in your sight in sin.
Put forth to me the power of your love,
     be leaping over the mountains of my transgressions,
     and wash me in the true blood of conciliation.

A Hymn, sung or heard (optional)

Pray I this day my prayer to you, my loving Lord.
This and each day I remember the source of the mercies
you have bestowed on me gently and generously.
     This and each day I pray to be fuller in love to you.
O Blessed Lamb, lift me up from the state of death,
     from the state of torments to the state of grace,
     to the holy state of the high heavens.
O Blessed Lamb, take charge of my soul,
     with your loving arm about my body,
     through each moment of my life.
May the cross of your crucifixion tree,
sore and heavy upon your wounded back,
     deliver me from distress and from death.
May the cross of your crucifixion tree,
which you bore without fault,
     be outstretched towards me in love.
Jesus! Lamb of God and only-begotten Son of the Father,
     you gave the wine-blood of your body

to buy me from the grave.
Jesus! Be near me, uphold me, my treasure, my triumph,
        in my lying, in my standing,
        in my watching, in my sleeping,
O Blessed Lamb, take charge of my soul,
        with your loving arm about my body,
        through each moment of my life.
O Blessed Lamb, lift me up from the state of death,
        from the state of torments to the state of grace,
        to the holy state of the high heavens.
Place I in you my hope, O loving Lord,
that I may walk without fault in this world
        and be with you in the distant world to come.

A Psalm, read or recited

Lord Jesus Christ,
Lamb of God and God of all Glory,
guide me with your wisdom,
        chastise me with your justice,
help me with your mercy,
        protect me with your strength.

A Scriptural Reading, read aloud or quietly

Lord Jesus Christ,
Lamb of God and God of all Glory,
fill me with your fullness,
        shield me with your shade,
fill me with your grace,
        for the sake of your love everlasting.

Lord Jesus Christ,
Lamb of God and God of all Glory,
who was hanged upon the tree,
pour down upon me from heaven
the rich blessing of your forgiveness.
        Be patient with me and pour down
        the rich blessing of your loving providence.
Each day and each night remember I your covenant;

in my lying down and rising up I yield to your cross.
Each thing I have received, from you it came,
each thing for which I hope, from your love it will come,
    each thing I enjoy, it is of your bounty,
    each thing I asked, comes from your disposing.
Forgive my faults and failings, relieving my burdens,
    that I may embrace and accept your love.
Bestow upon me the faith of the angels and the saints,
    that I may love and serve you in this life.
Vouchsafe to me a mansion in the realm of peace,
    that I may love and serve you in the life to come.
O Lamb of God and Word Everlasting,
grant me to have this living prayer:
    enlighten my understanding, kindle my will, begin my doing,
    incite my love, strengthen my weakness, enfold my desire.
Cleanse my heart, make holy my soul, confirm my faith,
    keep safe my mind and compass my body about.
As I utter this prayer from my mouth,
    in my own heart may I feel your presence.
O Lamb of God and Word Everlasting,
grant that you will be always at my breast, will be always at my back,
    grant that you will give me my needs as may befit the crown
    you have promised to me in the world beyond.

Lord Jesus Christ,
Lamb of God and God of all Glory,
be with me on this your day,
    Amen.
Be with me on this your night,
    Amen.
Anything that is evil to me,
or that may witness against me
where I shall longest be,
    illume it to me,
    banish it from me,
    root it out of my heart,
    ever, ever more, everlastingly.

Select one of the following options for the Lord's Prayer.

Option A

O Lord, Lamb of God,
son of God and son of Mary,
help me pray as you yourself taught:
>"Our Father in heaven,
>hallowed be your name.
>Your kingdom come.
>Your will be done,
>on earth as it is in heaven.
>Give us this day our daily bread.
>And forgive us our debts,
>as we also have forgiven our debtors.
>And do not bring us to the time of trial,
>but rescue us from the evil one."
>(Matthew 6: 9-13)
Thanks be to my Eternal Father,
who has enwrapped my body and my soul,
>safeguarding me in the sanctuary of his love
>and sheltering me under the mantle of his care.
Thanks be to you, Eternal Father,
>For the kingdom, and the power, and the glory,
>are yours for ever and ever. Amen.

*Please proceed with "The peace of Christ, the Lamb of God...," found
after Option B.*

Option B

O Lord, Lamb of God,
son of God and son of Mary,
help me pray as you yourself taught:
>Our Father in heaven,
>hallowed be your name,
>your kingdom come,
>your will be done,
>on earth as in heaven.
>Give us today our daily bread.
>Forgive us our sins
>as we forgive those who sin against us.

Lead us not into temptation
but deliver us from evil.
Thanks be to my Eternal Father,
who has enwrapped my body and my soul,
   safeguarding me in the sanctuary of his love
   and sheltering me under the mantle of his care.
Thanks be to you, Eternal Father,
   For the kingdom, and the power, and the glory,
   are yours for ever and ever. Amen.

The peace of Christ, the Lamb of God,
be upon each thing my eye takes in,
upon my body that is of earth
and upon my soul that came from on high,
   upon my body that is of earth
   and upon my soul that came from on high.
Bless, O holy Lord, my face,
let my face bless everything;
   bless, O holy Lord, my eye,
   let my eye bless all it sees.
The peace of Christ be to me,
during all my life,
during all the days of my life.
   The peace of Christ be to all,
   during all their lives,
   during all the days of their lives.

A Hymn, sung or heard (optional)

Jesus, give me forgiveness of sins,
Jesus, keep my guilt in my memory,
Jesus, give me the grace of repentance,
Jesus, give me the grace of forgiveness,
   Jesus give me the grace of submission,
   Jesus, give me the grace of earnestness,
   Jesus, give me the grace of lowliness.
Jesus, take pity upon me,
Jesus, have mercy upon me,
   Jesus, take me to you,
   Jesus, aid my soul

End this time of prayer by taking some time to bring to mind the ways you disregard God's desires or hurt others before contemplating the depth of God's love and forgiveness. Then, when you are ready, conclude by saying:

I am bending my knee
in the eye of the Father who created me,
in the eye of the Son who purchased me,
in the eye of the Spirit who cleansed me,
in friendship and affection. Amen.

Devotional Exercises

Considerations

These exercises are designed to become habits of prayer that remain integrated into your daily life, rather than moments where you put your daily concerns aside to pray. Because of this, individuals approaching these devotions will find it helpful to:

• Memorize the Core Prayers from the *Carmina Gadelica*
It will be useful to memorize the central prayers used in each of these exercises, in much the same way that the original men and women who composed these prayers used them in their own lives. While this may seem a bit daunting, be assured that the rhythm of the prayers makes it possible to memorize them quite easily.

However, individuals who are not able to memorize these prayers may write them on a small card or place them in a notepad on their mobile phone so that they may consult them when they are needed. But it is important to record only the prayers so that the surrounding exercises become natural to each individual person.

• Make These Exercises Unique to Themselves
The instructions for these exercises are not intended to be a rigid set of rules. Instead, they are designed to help individuals create a framework which will ultimately be adapted to their particular needs. Each person will need to decide how much time to devote to the exercises as well as how much to each particular part of it.

Individuals may find that certain parts of the exercises may move slightly, depending on their own desires and needs. Trust that God is present in these decisions and will make the exercises unique gifts to each individual person.

With these concerns in mind, it also would be helpful for individuals to:

• Integrate the Examens into their Daily Routines
While many people set aside 10-15 minutes in a quiet space to conduct the examen, individuals may find it better to coordinate their prayerful consideration of the day — either that which is coming or which has already passed — to a daily activity, such as dressing and

undressing (i.e., putting on and taking off the concerns of the day). This will take time and effort since routine daily activities are often filled with distractions, but the effort will be rewarded since the individual will always have time devoted to the examen while also rendering that daily activity sacred.

• Choose the Appropriate Prayer Rope or Beads
The Orthodox Christian church uses various types of prayer ropes, with the most common being one with about 100 knots that is usually wrapped around the left wrist until it is needed for prayer. But the Pilgrim's Prayer Rope described in this prayerbook is best conducted using a much smaller version with 30 knots between two beads and an knotted cross. This allows an individual to decide whether to use the prayer rope for a short time (i.e., between 10-15 minutes for each cycle of the prayer rope) or to continue the prayers over a longer period.

Note: These smaller prayer ropes may be purchased from Orthodox churches or from monasteries and convents in the Orthodox tradition. Some of the monasteries and convents that sell these prayer ropes have websites.

Another option would be to use Anglican prayer beads (sometimes called a rosary) in the manner described in this section. It is important to note that this approach does not follow the conventional use of these beads, which may be explained in materials provided with the beads when they are purchased.

The prayers in these descriptions also may be adapted to other types of prayer beads, especially those from other religious traditions. However, this will require prayerful consideration of the rhythms of prayer established in this exercise so that the person finds the best way to use these prayers with another devotional aid.

Making a Morning Caim

a prayerful consideration of the coming day

[1]   Focus on this present moment and allow all other concerns or problems to fade from your consciousness. Then, become aware of your desire to know the fullness of God's love for you — and to feel his continuing compassion and guidance — as you quietly affirm God's redemptive presence in you and in the world around you.

[2]   Consider your life. Bring to mind the times when you do not reflect God's goodness, the times when you squander or misuse the gifts he has given to you, and the times when you feel abandoned by God. Become aware of your desire to live in God's goodness as well as your desire to properly use the many gifts he has given you.

[3]   Pray for the grace to see God's action in your life more clearly, to understand his desires for you more accurately, to respond to his guidance to you more generously. Pray also that others in the world might see, understand and respond to God's guidance in their lives.

[4]   Now, imagine the coming day, seeing God's love enfolding and encircling every situation. Feel God's love touch you in the depths of your being, expressing his desire to share his creation with you in the coming day. Ask God to bless your day, the people and creatures you will meet in it, and those who are close to your heart.

• Then, see God in all the events and people of the coming morning. Feel his loving presence surrounding, protecting and guiding you as you imagine the moments when you expect to be alone during this morning and when you expect to be with other people. Feel God's love pervade your home, your work and your travels as you ask him to encircle the events and people of this morning with his love, saying:

The compassing of God be on you,
The compassing of the God of life.

• Imagine the events and people of the coming midday. Again, feel God's presence surrounding, protecting and guiding you as you see the moments when you expect to be alone and when you expect to be with other people. As you ask him to encircle the events and people of this midday with his love, saying:

The compassing of Christ be on you,
The compassing of the Christ of love.

• Envision the coming afternoon, seeing God's presence in the times when you are alone and when you are with others. Hear his voice speak to you in all these events and people as you ask God to encircle them with his love, saying:

The compassing of Spirit be on you,
The compassing of the Spirit of Grace.

• Finally, see the coming evening. Feel God's love pervade the moments when you expect to be alone and when you expect to be with other people before asking him to encircle them with his love, saying:

The compassing of the Three be on you,
The compassing of the Three preserve you,
The compassing of the Three preserve you.

[5]   As you allow these images to ebb and flow in your consciousness, make a mental note of your emotional responses to the people and events you expect to encounter during the coming day, quietly affirming your desire to live in God's goodness. Then, become aware of your need for God's continuing care and guidance so you may properly use the many gifts he has given you in these circumstances — and in the unexpected events of this day.

[6]   When you are ready, conclude by offering this traditional prayer:

God, bless to me the new day,
Never vouchsafed to me before;
It is to bless your own presence
Thou hast given me this time, O God.
Bless my eye,
may my eye bless all it sees;
I will bless my neighbor,
May my neighbor bless me.
God, give me a clean heart,
let me not from sight of your eye. Amen.

An Evening Prayer of Remembrance

venerating God's presence in the passing day

[1]   Become completely focused on this present moment and allow all other concerns or problems to dissolve from your consciousness. Become aware of God's goodness and of the many gifts that God has given to you, quietly acknowledging God's sustaining power in your life and in the world around you.

[2]   Consider your life. Bring to mind the times when you do not reflect God's goodness, the times when you squander or misuse the gifts God has given to you, and the times when you feel abandoned by God. Become aware of your desire to live in God's goodness and quietly affirm your desire to properly use the many gifts God has given you, asking for God's continuing guidance to help you achieve this goal.

[3]   Become aware of the need — both in you and in the world around you — for God's healing and redemptive presence.

• Open yourself to that divine presence as you ponder and pray the words of this traditional prayer:

I am bending my knee
In the eye of the Father who created me,
In the eye of the Son who purchased me,
In the eye of the Spirit who cleansed me,
In friendship and affection.

• Then, pray for the grace to see God's action in your life more clearly, to understand God's desires for you more accurately, and to respond to God's guidance to you more generously. Pray also that others in the world might see, understand and respond to God's guidance in their lives.

[4]   Now, review this day in your memory, allowing yourself to feel God's presence in its events and emotions.

• Remember waking this morning. Recall whether you awoke easily or with difficulty, calling to mind how you felt — whether you were happy, sad, relaxed or tense. Make a mental note of whether you felt God close to you or distant from you. Take a moment to consider these things, acknowledging the shaping presence of God in the beginning of the day, as you say:

I am bending my knee

In friendship and affection.

• Recall your preparations for the day. Remember whether you dressed quickly or slowly, calling to mind your thoughts and feelings. Ask yourself whether God was on your mind as you prepared for this day. Take a moment to consider any feelings that these memories evoke in you, acknowledging the shaping presence of God in them, as you say:

I am bending my knee
In friendship and affection.

• Bring to mind your morning. Recall those moments when you were alone and when you were with other people. Recall the emotions you felt during the morning hours, allowing specific feelings to connect to the things you did as well as the things about which you thought or talked. Ask yourself how God was present to you this morning. Take a moment to consider these images and feelings, acknowledging the shaping presence of God in them, as you say:

I am bending my knee
In friendship and affection.

• Call to mind what you did at midday, remembering those moments when you were alone and when you were with other people, becoming aware of any emotions associated with specific things you did or things about which you thought or talked. Ask yourself about the ways in which God was present to you or on your mind at midday. Take a moment to consider these images and feelings, acknowledging the shaping presence of God in them, as you say:

I am bending my knee
In friendship and affection.

• Remember your afternoon, recalling those moments when you were alone and when you were with other people. Recall the emotions you felt during the afternoon, particularly if they are connected to specific things you did or about which you thought or talked. Ask yourself how God was present to you this afternoon. Take a moment to consider these images and feelings, acknowledging the shaping presence of God in them, as you say:

I am bending my knee
In friendship and affection.

• Recall your evening, remembering those moments when you were alone and when you were with other people. Become aware of any emotions you felt during the evening hours as you consider the things you did as well as the things about which you thought or talked.

Ask yourself how God revealed his presence to you this evening. Take a moment to consider these images and feelings, acknowledging the shaping presence of God in them, as you say:

> *I am bending my knee*
> *In friendship and affection.*

• Consider the present moment. Become aware of your feelings and your current sense of God's presence. Take a moment to consider these feelings, acknowledging the shaping presence of God in this moment, as you say:

> *I am bending my knee*
> *In friendship and affection.*

[5]   Allow all the images and memories to flow freely in your consciousness, feeling God's presence in them. Make a mental note of your emotional responses to these images and memories as they ebb and flow. Then, become aware once again of your desire to live in God's goodness as you quietly affirm your desire to properly use the many gifts he has given you and ask for his continued guidance as you try to achieve this goal.

[6]   When you are ready, conclude with this traditional prayer:

> *Through your own Anointed One, O God,*
> *Bestow upon us fullness in our need.*
>> *Love towards God,*
>> *The affection of God,*
>> *The smile of God,*
>> *The wisdom of God,*
>> *The grace of God,*
>> *The fear of God*
> *To do in the world of the Three,*
> *As angels and saints*
> *Do in heaven;*
>> *Each shade and light,*
>> *Each day and night,*
>> *Each time in kindness,*
>> *Give us your Spirit. Amen.*

A Pilgrim's Prayer Cycle

using a prayer rope

[1]   Focus on this present moment and allow all other concerns or problems to fade from your consciousness. Then, become aware of your desire to know the fullness of God's love for you — and to feel his continuing compassion and guidance — as you quietly affirm God's redemptive presence in you and in the world around you.

[2]   Hold one of the outer knots on your prayer rope's cross. Beginning from that knot, mark the sign of the cross using the other outer knots of the cross on your prayer rope as you say:

> *I am bending my knee*
> *In the eye of the Father who created me,*
> *In the eye of the Son who purchased me,*
> *In the eye of the Spirit who cleansed me*
> > *in friendship and affection.*

• Afterward, place any special concerns or desires you have before the Trinity in a brief prayer of offering. Or, if you have any pressing questions that you want answered, ask them of the Lord in a brief petitionary prayer.

[3]   Now, holding the central knot of the cross, pray slowly:

> *My God and my Chief,*
> *I seek you in the morning,*
> *My God and my Chief,*
> *I seek you this night.*
> *I am giving you my mind,*
> *I am giving you my will,*
> *I am giving you my wish,*
> *My soul everlasting and my body.*
> > *May you be chieftain over me,*
> > *May you be master unto me,*
> > *May you be shepherd over me,*
> > *May you be guardian unto me,*
> > *May you be herdsmen over me,*
> > *May you be guide unto me,*
> > *May you be with me, O Chief of chiefs,*
> > *Father everlasting and God of the heavens.*

[4]   Then, going in either direction from the knotted cross, hold one of the beads as you pray:

> *God and Jesus and the Spirit of cleansing*
> *Be shielding me, be possessing me, be aiding me,*
> *Be clearing my path and going before my soul*
> *In hollow, on hill, on plain,*
> *On sea and on land be the Three aiding me.*

• Ask for the grace to see God's action in your life more clearly, to understand his desires for you more accurately, to respond to his guidance to you more generously. Pray also that others in the world might see, understand and respond to God's guidance in their lives.

Note: If your prayer rope does not have these beads next to the knotted cross, complete this step while still holding the cross.

[5]   Take a moment to decide what you desire from God — protection, forgiveness or guidance — and decide which of the following petitions you want to use during your prayer:

For Protection

> *O Jesus, a shade are you in the heat,*
> *A shelter are you in the cold*
> *An island are you at sea,*
> *A fortress are you on land,*
> *A well are you in the desert.*
> > *O Jesus! in your strength*
> > *Preserve me.*

For Forgiveness

> *O Jesus, give me the forgiveness of sins,*
> *Keep my guilt in my memory,*
> *Give me the grace of repentance,*
> *Give me the grace of forgiveness,*
> *Give me the grace of humility,*
> *O Jesus, take pity on me,*
> > *Jesus, aid my soul.*

For Guidance

> *O Holy God, guide me with your wisdom,*
> *Chastise me with your justice,*

Help me with your mercy,
Protect me with your strength,
Fill me with your grace, O God,
For the sake of your anointed son.

Note: If your prayer rope does not have a bead next to the cross, you also should decide at this point which direction you wish to go as you proceed around the rope.

[6]   Then, hold the knot next to the bead and say the first line of the petition. Holding each of the following knots in turn, say the corresponding line from the petition — the second line while holding the second knot, the third line while holding the third knot, and so forth — until you reach the fifth knot. While holding the fifth knot, recite the fifth line <u>and</u> the final coda from the petition before proceeding to the next knot and beginning the cycle anew.

Note: If you are using a larger prayer rope, you may encounter beads as you proceed around the rope (usually after each tenth or fifteenth knot). If you do, pause for a moment and ask — in a quick prayer — for the grace you are requesting in this time of prayer.

• Continue this process until you reach the bead next to the knotted cross. Then, hold that bead (or continue holding the final knot on the circlet if you rope does not have this bead) and decide whether you wish to finish your prayer or continue.
     • **If you wish to continue praying**, take a moment to quietly reflect on your prayer and ask in a brief petition for the grace you are seeking during this time of prayer. Then, hold the knot next to the bead so that you reverse the direction around the circlet as you pray. You should continue in your usual manner until you come to the bead next to the cross again where you may again decide whether to continue (by repeating this process) or to conclude your prayer.
(*This process offers the opportunity to end the prayer period whenever you reach the bead at the end of the cycle. But it is very important not to go beyond either a predetermined number of cycles or a specific prayer time.*)
•   **If you wish to end your prayer period**, proceed to the next step.
[7]   Now, hold the bead as you pray:
          God and Jesus and the Spirit of cleansing

> Be shielding me, be possessing me, be aiding me,
> Be clearing my path and going before my soul
> In hollow, on hill, on plain,
> On sea and on land be the Three aiding me.

[8]   While again holding the central knot of the cross, pray slowly:
> My God and my Chief,
> I seek you in the morning,
> My God and my Chief,
> I seek you this night.
> I am giving you my mind,
> I am giving you my will,
> I am giving you my wish,
> My soul everlasting and my body.
>> May you be chieftain over me,
>> May you be master unto me,
>> May you be shepherd over me,
>> May you be guardian unto me,
>> May you be herdsmen over me,
>> May you be guide unto me,
>> May you be with me, O Chief of chiefs,
>> Father everlasting and God of the heavens.

[9]   Once again, hold one of the outer knots on your prayer rope's cross. Beginning from that knot, conclude your by marking the sign of the cross with the other outer knots of the cross as you say:
> I am bending my knee
> In the eye of the Father who created me,
> In the eye of the Son who purchased me,
> In the eye of the Spirit who cleansed me
>> in friendship and affection. Amen.

A Pilgrim's Prayer Cycle

_____

using prayer beads

[1]   Focus on this present moment and allow all other concerns or problems to fade from your consciousness. Then, become aware of your desire to know the fullness of God's love for you — and to feel his continuing compassion and guidance — as you quietly affirm God's redemptive presence in you and in the world around you.

   Note: _The Anglican prayer beads used in this exercise have a cross at the end of a cord containing two additional beads that join a larger circlet containing four groups of seven beads separated by three distinctive (and usually larger) beads. If the beads you use are different from this, you may need to adapt the prayers in this exercise._

[2]   When you are ready, hold the top of the cross and mark the sign of the cross by touching or holding the other arms as you say:
> _I am bending my knee_
> _In the eye of the Father who created me,_
> _In the eye of the Son who purchased me,_
> _In the eye of the Spirit who cleansed me._
> _in friendship and affection_

   • Afterward, place any special concerns or desires you have before the Trinity in a brief prayer of offering. Or, if you have any pressing questions that you want answered, ask them of the Lord in a brief petitionary prayer.

[3]   Now, holding the bead directly above the cross, pray slowly:
> _My God and my Chief,_
> _I seek you in the morning,_
> _My God and my Chief,_
> _I seek you this night._
> _I am giving you my mind,_
> _I am giving you my will,_
> _I am giving you my wish,_
> _My soul everlasting and my body._
>> _May you be chieftain over me,_
>> _May you be master unto me,_
>> _May you be shepherd over me,_

May you be guardian unto me,
May you be herdsmen over me,
May you be guide unto me,
May you be with me, O Chief of chiefs,
Father everlasting and God of the heavens.

[4]   Then, hold the next bead as you pray:
God and Jesus and the Spirit of cleansing
Be shielding me, be possessing me, be aiding me,
Be clearing my path and going before my soul
In hollow, on hill, on plain,
On sea and on land be the Three aiding me.

• Ask for the grace to see God's action in your life more clearly, to understand his desires for you more accurately, to respond to his guidance to you more generously. Pray also that others in the world might see, understand and respond to God's guidance in their lives.

[5]   Take a moment to decide what you desire from God — protection, forgiveness or guidance — and decide which of the following petitions you want to use during your prayer:

<u>For Protection</u>
O Jesus, a shade are you in the heat,
A shelter are you in the cold,
Eyes are you to the blind,
A staff are you to the pilgrim,
An island are you at sea,
A fortress are you on land,
A well are you in the desert.
            O Jesus! in your strength
            Preserve me.

<u>For Forgiveness</u>
O Jesus, give me the forgiveness of sins,
Keep my guilt in my memory,
Give me the grace of repentance,
Give me the grace of forgiveness,
Give me the grace of submission.
Give me the grace of earnestness,
Give me the grace of humility,
O Jesus, take pity on me,
            Jesus, aid my soul.

For Guidance
O Holy God, guide me with your wisdom,
Chastise me with your justice,
Help me with your mercy,
Protect me with your strength,
Nourish me with your fullness,
Shield me with your shade,
Fill me with your grace, O God,
For the sake of your anointed son.

• You now should take a moment to decide which way you will proceed around the main circlet as you use these petitions.

[6]   When you are ready, hold the first bead on the circlet and say the first line of the petition. Holding each of the following beads in turn, say the corresponding line from the petition — the second line while holding the second bead, the third line while holding the third bead, and so forth — until you reach the first distinctive bead. Now, holding that bead, say the final coda from the petition before proceeding to the next series of beads and beginning the cycle anew.

• Continue this process until you reach the final bead in the fourth series. Then, hold the top bead from the strand leading to the cross and decide whether you wish to finish your prayer or continue.

• **If you want to continue praying**, say the final coda from your petition as you would with the other distinctive beads and then return to the main circlet in the opposite direction to what you have previously been praying. You should continue in your usual manner until you come to the first bead on the strand containing the cross again where you may again decide whether to continue (by repeating this process) or to end your prayer time.

(This process offers the opportunity to end the prayer period whenever you reach the bead at the end of the cycle. But it is very important not to go beyond either a predetermined number of cycles or a specific prayer time.)

• **If you wish to end your prayer period**, proceed to the next step.

[7]   Now, hold the top bead from the strand leading to the cross as you pray:

God and Jesus and the Spirit of cleansing

> *Be shielding me, be possessing me, be aiding me,*
> *Be clearing my path and going before my soul*
> *In hollow, on hill, on plain,*
> *On sea and on land be the Three aiding me.*

[8} Holding the bead next to the cross, pray slowly:

> *My God and my Chief,*
> *I seek you in the morning,*
> *My God and my Chief,*
> *I seek you this night.*
> *I am giving you my mind,*
> *I am giving you my will,*
> *I am giving you my wish,*
> *My soul everlasting and my body.*
>> *May you be chieftain over me,*
>> *May you be master unto me,*
>> *May you be shepherd over me,*
>> *May you be guardian unto me,*
>> *May you be herdsmen over me,*
>> *May you be guide unto me,*
>> *May you be with me, O Chief of chiefs,*
>> *Father everlasting and God of the heavens.*

[9] Finally, conclude by again holding the top of the cross while marking the sign of the cross by touching or holding the remaining arms as you say:

> *I am bending my knee*
> *In the eye of the Father who created me,*
> *In the eye of the Son who purchased me,*
> *In the eye of the Spirit who cleansed me.*
>> *in friendship and affection. Amen.*

Resources

for the Liturgy and Sequences

The prayerful experience of the Carmichael Liturgy and prayer sequences will be shaped by the readings used in them. Most of these readings will come from the Bible, so it is important that individuals and groups decide how they wish to select these scriptural selections.

For individuals and communities using the Carmichael Liturgy and prayer sequences on a regular basis, it might be best to link their prayers to a larger church community by using the cycles of reading developed by various churches. On the other hand, if the liturgy and sequences are being used for a special occasion, they may want to select specific readings that will create services devoted to particular themes.

Using Cycles of Scriptural Readings

Many churches have regular cycles of readings that are used to ensure that different church communities share in a common life of prayer. The cycles may be found in the lectionaries adopted and published by the different churches. In the Roman Catholic Church, the readings for Sunday follow a three-year cycle and weekday readings use a two-year cycle. On the other hand, many Protestant churches use the Revised Common Lectionary which has a three-year cycle for both Sunday and weekday readings. While the Roman Catholic lectionary always includes a Gospel reading, the Revised Common Lectionary does not always use a Gospel reading during the week.

Note: *The Revised Common Lectionary also includes two "tracks". Track One uses secondary readings that usually focus on their own themes and narratives, whereas Track Two follows the Roman Catholic tradition of coordinating secondary readings to the Gospel.*

In addition to the Revised Common Lectionary, many Protestant churches have created their own guidelines with regard to scriptural readings (including additional selections that may be used at services particular to their own denomination). So, individuals and groups who want to link the Carmichael Liturgy and prayer sequences to a larger church community's experience of the Scriptures may wish to consult local church bulletins to find the readings of the day being used in them.

For individuals and groups who do not want to use the lectionaries of various churches, an alternative way of creating scriptural continuity between different uses of the Carmichael Liturgy or the prayer sequences would be to follow particular biblical narratives from one time of prayer to the next. This would involve choosing a particular Gospel — as well as deciding which selections from that Gospel to use — before incorporating these choices into the liturgy and sequences. While this involves a greater commitment of time and effort than using an existing lectionary, it also offers individuals and groups with a deeper experience of the Scriptures during their prayer.

Choosing Thematic Biblical Readings

Finding scriptural passages on particular themes requires greater time and effort then using the lectionary or biblical cycles, but it also enriches the Carmichael Liturgy and prayer sequences by allowing individuals and groups to prayerfully focus on their specific needs and concerns. The best way to ensure that thematic readings speak most effectively during prayer involve knowing how they affect people in prayer, so it is important to carefully review any scriptural reading and discover the significance of these readings when used with the liturgy or sequences.

One approach to finding these readings involves carefully consulting the resources prepared by other people, such as online websites and biblical concordances (whether online or in print). An online search on a particular topic (e.g., "God's guidance Bible verse") will provide some choices for thematic biblical readings, probably a list of specific biblical verses containing the words "God" and "guidance". But using a concordance should provide a broader context for the theme within the Bible, usually suggesting readings related to different types of guidance God might offer. It will be important that the individuals selecting thematic readings for the liturgy or sequences take time to compare biblical verses so that they properly address the desires presented in prayer.

Another way of finding thematic scriptural readings involves delving into people's previous encounters with the Bible to find passages that have offered consolation or inspiration in the past. Individuals approaching the prayer sequences should take the time to consider scriptural selections that are meaningful to them and determine how these passages might contribute to their prayer. Prayer groups approaching the Carmichael Liturgy and prayer sequences also might collect favorite scriptural passages from among their members before compiling a list of thematic selections for use in their prayers.

Note: Individuals who are new to prayer using biblical readings might consult trusted friends or spiritual guides to ask for their favorite scriptural passages as well as the reasons why these selections became significant. It also might be helpful to consult the suggestions for the thematic prayer sequences in the following table.

Topic	Psalms	Other Readings
God's Guidance	Psalm 23 Psalm 112 Psalm 119	John 14: 15-27 1 Corinthians 13: 1-13 Galatians 5: 13-26
God's Protection	Psalm 27 Psalm 62 Psalm 91	Isaiah 61: 1-11 Luke 12: 22-31 Romans 8: 18-30
God's Consolation	Psalm 40 Psalm 118 Psalm 139	Jeremiah 29: 11-14 John 4: 1-26 Ephesians 1: 3-14
God's Forgiveness	Psalm 36 Psalm 51 Psalm 145	Luke 15: 11-32 John 3: 16-21 Colossians 1: 15-23

God's Call	Psalm 18 Psalm 37 Psalm 61	Jeremiah 1: 4-10 Matthew 16: 24-27 Romans 12: 9-21

Regardless of how individuals or groups find the thematic selections they use in the Carmichael Liturgy and prayer sequences, it is important to remember that knowing how scriptural selections might affect people — both emotionally and intellectually — remains the best way to ensure that thematic readings speak most effectively during prayer. So, take time to consider any biblical passage before including it in the liturgy or sequences.

Selecting Reflective Readings for the Carmichael Liturgy

Finding readings for the Carmichael Liturgy's prelude requires special care. It is important that any reflective selection prior to the liturgy invite the community members into a calm and contemplative atmosphere of prayer and not provoke them to think about the issues of the reading. With this in mind, the readings selected for the prelude — whether they are scriptural selections, excerpts from a spiritual writer or poems — should be relatively brief and poetic in character when compared to the Gospel presented later in the liturgy.

More than with the selection of other thematic biblical readings, the spiritual impact of the reflective readings for the Carmichael Liturgy's prelude should be carefully considered before they are included in the liturgy. It might be helpful for those individuals responsible for preparing the liturgy to share spiritual selections that have proven to be inspirational or consoling in the past. Then, with the other members of this group, the passages should be discussed reflectively — and delicately, so as to not hurt those for whom the reading is significant.

Since the purpose of this reading is to provide a foundation for the prayers to come, the reading chosen for the prelude should be connected either to the psalm or the Gospel used during the liturgy. Consequently, it may be either a secondary reading from a lectionary or another passage containing echoes of the later scriptural selections. But do not be afraid to trust spiritual leadings which place seemingly different selections together since quite often "God writes straight with curving lines".

Like the prayers collected in the *Carmina Gadelica*, the spiritual readings brought into the Carmichael Liturgy and prayer sequences — whether scriptural or not — carry with them generations of voices reaching out to God in faithful prayer. So, when carefully chosen, these selections in the liturgy and sequences will resonate with the words of the men and women whose own devotions were collected by Alexander Carmichael as well as with the invocations of God's grace expressed by modern-day worshipers.

With this in mind, the passages selected for the liturgy and sequences should preserve a delicate balance between speaking the needs of the people praying with them in the present and listening for the prayers of others from the past expressed in the readings. This requires maintaining a contemplative silence around the selections that allows the individuals praying the liturgy and sequences to remain receptive to these other voices — both of the generations of different Christians and of the Triune God drawing these diverse voices into the single Body of Christ — without losing an awareness of their own needs or of their own contribution to the ongoing prayer of the Church.

So, both in selecting the readings for the Carmichael Liturgy or prayer sequences and in subsequently offering them in worship, listening for the voices of others in these passages will provide spiritual gifts during both their preparation and their prayerful presentation during the liturgy or the sequences. It is a double blessing that should be recognized with gratitude and approached with reverence.

with the Liturgy and Sequences

While music is not essential to the Carmichael Liturgy or the prayer sequences, it does offer an additional layer of prayerfulness as it opens individuals to contemplation and provides additional words for worship. So, it is important for individuals and groups approaching the liturgy and sequences to decide if they wish to incorporate music and song into their prayer as well as determine what types of music are best suited to their needs.

Sources for Songs and Music

Although individuals and communities may wish to use different types of music with this prayerbook, the rhythms and language of the Carmichael Liturgy and prayer sequences invite the use of Celtic hymns and songs. So, it is fortunate that there are a number of published collections of Celtic hymns and songs available. The Iona Community's Wild Goose Resource Group has published many songbooks that could be used with the prayer service and sequences presented in this book, and Ray Simpson (the Founding Guardian of the Community of Aidan and Hilda) has gathered 255 hymns — including both ancient and modern songs — in his *Celtic Hymn Book*. Also, a number of individual musicians and composers (such as George Bayley, Roddy Cowie and Larry Shackley) have published or posted their own collections of Celtic/Gaelic-inspired music for prayer and worship that may be found through online searches.

For groups wanting to perform music during the services or sequences, the popularity of Celtic music ensures that scores are readily available for performers in general music stores. Although this music is predominantly secular, the popularity of Celtic Christianity among various churches has also led to musical scores of hymns and religious songs being available in music stores catering to religious groups.

Finally, there are a wide number of musical artists to have recorded musical versions of Celtic songs and hymns that may be presented electronically during the Carmichael Liturgy and prayer sequences.

Using Music to Foster Reflection during the Carmichael Liturgy

The Carmichael Liturgy promotes contemplation through its invitations to silent reflection, but a community may find it necessary to use instrumental music during these moments if its members find these proposed periods of silence too challenging. If this is the case, then care should be taken to ensure that the music does not become distracting or detract from the reflective character of the service.

One moment of special concern should be the service's prelude. Ideally, the prelude should involve the reading of a reflective selection (scriptural or inspirational) or the singing of a thematic song followed by a prolonged period of silent reflection. But if the community feels uneasy about the suggested silence, it might be better to begin by playing a short selection of quiet instrumental music before (and possibly during) the reading and then follow it with more music. Alternatively, a song might simply be followed by a prolonged period of instrumental music.

Another option during the prelude would be to play instrumental music throughout, whether performed live by musicians or presented through recordings. If this is the case, the music should be presented in a seamless manner that enhances the community's sense of reflective stillness.

Choosing and Using Songs for the Carmichael Liturgy

When considering the songs and hymns used during the Carmichael Liturgy, it is important to reflect on their place within the service. Depending on whether a community uses the Eucharistic Prayer, the liturgy offers the choice of singing on two or three occasions — at the end of the Word of God section and at the conclusion of the prayer services as well as at the end of the optional Eucharistic Prayer (when it is used). Each of these moments have their own particular character and this should be respected in the songs chosen for the service.

For instance:

• After the Word of God, it might be best to select a song that echoes the gospel reading or psalm used in that particular service — reaffirming the message of these scriptural passages at the heart of the community's reflections.

• On the other hand, a general thematic song would re-encapsulate the core message of the shared prayers at the end of the service before the members of the community disperse.

• At the end of the Eucharistic Prayer, however, a group may choose either to reassert the central reading of the service by using a gospel-based song or to "set the tone" for the service's final prayers and blessings by selecting a thematic song.

After selecting the music and songs that are best-suited to the community's needs during the Carmichael Liturgy, it will be necessary to decide the best way to present the songs during the service. It would be best for the community to sing the songs, but this will require that the group leaders find ways to introduce the music and invite communal singing. If this is not possible, it might be best to create a small ensemble of musicians and singers to create a contemplative atmosphere during the service, allowing them to perform the songs for the community. Each community will need to decide which option works best for them.

Choosing and Using Songs for the Prayer Sequences

If the sequences are being used for community prayer, the group may want to sing hymns near the beginning and at the end of its time together. If being used for private devotions, or if the prayer group is unable to sing together, the person or group may wish to listen to favorite hymns or songs at these points during the sequences using recordings. If music is desired, these hymns and songs should reflect the character of the moment in the sequence where they are being used.

For instance:

• Songs and hymns used near the beginning of the sequence should be thematic, helping the individual or group enter into the coming prayer. For this reason, it might be best to select songs that either echo the general theme of the sequence (e.g., guidance, protection, forgiveness, etc.) or the readings being used during the sequence.

• On the other hand, songs and hymns at the end of the sequence should reflect the hopes and desires expressed during the previous prayers. For example, these songs might focus on expressions of gratitude, repentance or hope in God's continuing presence.

Like the thematic music used in the prelude to the Carmichael Liturgy, the songs and hymns used during the prayer sequences should facilitate reflective prayer and be selected so that they do not distract from the general contemplative atmosphere developed through the prayer sequences.

While hymns and songs are a form of prayer, there is always a need to balance the different dispositions cultivated by other expressions of worship. Both the Carmichael Liturgy and the prayer sequences benefit from the inclusion of music, but they also invite silent reflection and contemplation. With this in mind, the music used during these prayers should complement — rather than compete with — the overall structure of prayer.

So, cultivate familiarity with the music you select before presenting it in order that it may connect naturally with the spoken words and silent spaces in the prayer services. Individuals will already do this because they are selecting favorite hymns to use during their prayer. But prayer groups might consider offering the songs used during the liturgy and sequences to their members prior to their communal use, allowing them to germinate in each person in their own unique ways prior to the shared moments of worship.

Each person or community using music during the Carmichael Liturgy or during the prayer sequences will need to find their own way of preserving the balance between singing, speaking and listening that nurture the quiet and contemplative character of these prayer services. This demand poses a challenge, but it also offers great rewards.

rituals for creating a sacred space

The consequences of incorporating personal rituals into our prayer often exceed our expectations. The consistent use of private rituals helps us develop bodily habits that allow us to more quickly put aside our daily concerns and enter into a prayerful conversation with our Creator. But these rituals also remind us that we are invoking protection and guidance while seeking communion with a loving God. With each successive act of ritual, we invite God to consecrate our time with him and reconfirm our desire that he transform us into signs of his presence in the world.

With these goals in mind, you may find one or more of the following three rituals (using traditional Gaelic prayers selected from Alexander Carmichael's *Carmina Gadelica*) helpful:

#1 — A Trinitarian Act of Humility

Note: For this ritual, place three candles at the focal point of your prayer space — along with an image of the Trinity (e.g., a triskele or an icon), if you like. You also will need some matches or a long lighter.

• After relaxing into your prayer space, light the candles while reciting this prayer:

> *I am bending my knee*
> > (lighting the first candle)
> *in the eye of the Father who created me,*
> > (lighting the second candle)
> *in the eye of the Son who died for me,*
> > (lighting the third candle)
> *in the eye of the Spirit who cleansed me,*
> > *in love and desire.*

• After completing your prayer, as you prepare to leave your prayer space, extinguish the candles in the same order you originally lit them while repeating the following prayer:

> *I am bending my knee*
> *in the eye of the Father who created me,*

(extinguishing the first candle)
in the eye of the Son who died for me,
(extinguishing the second candle)
in the eye of the Spirit who cleansed me,
(extinguishing the third candle)
in love and desire. Amen.

#2 — A Personal Caim (Encircling Prayer)

Note: This ritual does not require any objects, but you may want to use a crucifix or other image of Jesus as the focal point of your prayer space.

• After becoming comfortable, open your hands — palms up — in front of you or pick up and hold the image of Jesus. Then, looking at your palms or the image, offer the following prayer:
>*O Lord, who brought me from the rest of last night*
>*Unto the joyous light of this day,*
>*Bring me from the new light of this day*
>*Unto the guiding light of eternity.*

• Now, allowing an image to form in your imagination as you slowly say:
>*The shape of Christ be towards me,*
>*The shape of Christ be from me,*
>*The shape of Christ be before me,*
>*The shape of Christ be behind me,*
>*The shape of Christ be over me,*
>*The shape of Christ be under me,*
>*The shape of Christ be with me,*
>*The shape of Christ be around me.*

• When you are finished, return the image of Jesus to its place or move your hands to where you will hold them during prayer.

• After you finish your prayer, pick up and hold the image of Jesus or open your hands in front of you as you pray:
>*O Lord, bring me from the new light of this day*
>*Unto the guiding light of eternity.*
>>*Oh! from the new light of this day*
>>*Unto the guiding light of eternity. Amen.*

• Wait a moment in silence after the prayer. Then, close your hands or replace the image of Jesus before leaving.

#3 — A Veneration of the Cross

Note: In this ritual, the focal point for your prayer space should include a candle placed before a cross or crucifix. You also will need some matches or a lighter.

- After calming yourself, make the sign of the cross while saying:
  > *In the name of the King of life,*
  > *In the name of the Christ of love,*
  > *In the name of the Holy Spirit,*
  > *The triune of my strength.*
- Then, light the candle before continuing with this prayer:
  > *May the cross of the crucifixion tree*
  > *Upon the wounded back of Christ*
  > *Deliver me from distress,*
  > *From death and from spells.*

  > *The cross of Christ without fault,*
  > *All outstretched toward me;*
  > *O God, bless me!*
- After concluding your prayer period, repeat the following prayer while you extinguish the candle:
  > *May the cross of the crucifixion tree*
  > *Upon the wounded back of Christ*
  > *Deliver me from distress,*
  > *From death and from spells.*

  > *The cross of Christ without fault,*
  > *All outstretched toward me;*
  > *O God, bless me!*
- Then, make the sign of the cross as you say:
  > *In the name of the King of life,*
  > *In the name of the Christ of love,*
  > *In the name of the Holy Spirit,*
  > *The triune of my strength. Amen.*

About the Author

A former Jesuit, **Timothy J. Ray** brings a diverse background in creative writing, cultural studies, theology and the history of ideas to his work in spiritual direction and formation. He received his Bachelor of Arts, *magna cum laude*, in a multi-disciplinary program focused on the cultural history of law and politics from Niagara University before earning, with distinction, both his Master of Fine Arts in Dramaturgy and Dramatic Criticism from Yale University and his Master of Letters in Theology from the University of Saint Andrews. In addition to preparing *The Carmichael Prayerbook*, he has published *A Journey to the Land of the Saints* and *A Pilgrimage to the Land of the Saints*.

For more information about Timothy and his activities, please visit http://www.silentheron.net.

68149705R00069